In Search of Thinness

WITHDRAWN
FROM
STOCK

616 · 8526

First published in 2008 by
CURRACH PRESS
55A Spruce Avenue, Stillorgan Industrial Park, Blackrock, Co. Dublin
www.currach.ie
1 3 5 4 2
Cover by sin é design
Origination by Currach Press
Printed in Ireland by ColourBooks, Baldoyle Industrial Estate, Dublin 13
ISBN: 978-1-85607-962-4

IN SEARCH OF THINNESS

TREATING ANOREXIA AND BULIMIA

A MULTI-DISCIPLINARY APPROACH

EDITED BY GILLIAN MOORE-GROARKE

CURRACH
PRESS

ACKNOWLEDGEMENTS

I would like to begin by thanking all of you who contributed to this book: Rory, Aisling, Ann Marie, Áine and Bríd. It has been my privilege to work with you all, and I appreciate your support over the years in working with many patients. A special word of thanks to my practice manager Deirdre Cashman.

This book would not have been possible without Jo O'Donoghue and her team at Currach Press. They placed their trust in us as professionals to come up with the goods.

I would also like to thank our patients and their families for supporting the treatment of eating disorders and for offering their stories to help educate others.

Thanks to Ted and his family for allowing their story to be printed and to Linda and Proinsias for their help at various stages of editing.

Finally I would like to thank my partner in life James and our daughter Jayne who continue to support me in all my work.

I hope this book helps sufferers and their families along the road of recovery.

Contents

Introduction

For the past eighteen years I have been working in the area of eating disorders. The first six years I spent working and training at the St Francis Medical Centre in Mullingar, before setting up the first out-patient clinic for eating disorders in Cork.

The shortage of beds and inappropriate in-patient facilities for sufferers of eating disorders have long since been a problem in Ireland. We have had no national survey with statistics about the exact numbers of sufferers. Although the government has set up the National Obesity Forum, to date there has been no increase in the number of hospital beds made available for sufferers from eating disorders.

In Cork I have been fortunate to have had the opportunity to work with many excellent general practitioners, psychiatrists, dietitians, physiotherapists, occupational therapists and addiction counsellors in order to promote a multi-disciplinary approach to the treatment of eating disorders. To their credit, the health professionals with whom I work every day provide the best they can for the patients under their care with minimal resources. For that I am very grateful, especially when patients have needed to be hospitalised and my concerns were taken up by their general practitioners and medical consultants.

I envisage that I will continue to work in this area but would dearly love to see funding provided for in-patient treatment facilities and appropriate out-patient programmes. Given the shortage of such facilities it is little wonder that those who cannot quickly access private treatment for themselves or their children air their grievances publicly.

There are many organisations and groups throughout this country – too many to list here but you know who you are – working in various ways but with one common aim: to alleviate the suffering of those with eating disorders. I applaud you all and your efforts. (A full resource list is included at the back of this book.)

I thank my colleagues here in Cork for writing this book with me and I also thank all my patients over the years who have placed their trust in me and my colleagues. I hope you find this book useful.

Gillian Moore-Groarke
Cork
May 2008

1

Eating Disorders in General Practice

Rory Lehane GP

By far the commonest eating disorder encountered in general practice (also referred to as primary care) is overeating. Overeating is officially classified as Binge Eating Disorder (BED). According to *The Merck Manual of Diagnosis and Therapy*[1], BED is characterised by binge-eating that is not followed by inappropriate compensatory behaviour such as self-induced vomiting or laxative abuse (as occurs in another eating disorder, bulimia nervosa).

Sometimes the person presenting to the general practitioner (GP) for consultation is primarily seeking help in losing weight but more often the subject of being overweight is brought up as part of a complex list of problems. This is what makes general practice both interesting and challenging – the fact that during a consultation any subject is likely to crop up, needing to be addressed there and then at the very least and, if possible, sorted out.

In order to calculate how overweight a person is we use the Body Mass Index (BMI). This is the person's weight measured in kilograms divided by the person's height in metres squared ($BMI=kg/m^2$). Non-overweight individuals have a BMI of between 20 and 25. Any person with a BMI of less than 20 is underweight and anybody with a BMI of between 25 and 30 is overweight, while those with a BMI of more than 30 are considered obese. Beyond this level again are different classes of severe obesity. These are linked to the risk of major illnesses such as high blood pressure, diabetes and heart disease.

Obesity is endemic in Ireland and affects both men and women equally. According to the Health Promotion Unit[2] and the *Report of the National Taskforce on Obesity*[3], obesity is one of the fastest-growing health problems in the country. One in eight Irish people is obese and every second person is overweight. The trends show that as a nation we are becoming progressively heavier - witnessed by the 30 per cent increase in reported obesity levels over the last four years.

Obesity is a direct consequence of overeating. Of course some uncommon medical conditions can contribute to obesity. The role of the GP is to test specifically for conditions that may have a medical basis and to treat them appropriately. These conditions include hypothyroidism, Cushing's syndrome and other hormonal disorders. Obesity may have its origins in childhood or may be a symptom of distress. It is well documented that persons who present with obesity may already have tried many diets without success. Research has shown that the more crash diets you undertake the more overweight you become.

So what are the challenges of Binge Eating Disorder for the GP? Can the GP measure everybody's BMI at every visit? No – the logistics alone prevent weight issues from being addressed at every consultation.

Let's look at a few scenarios:

SCENARIO 1

A lady in her early forties presents for consultation. (I say a lady because Irish men are notoriously unwilling to attend their GP.) She tells me that after having each of her three children she put on more weight which she can't seem to lose despite having tried numerous diets in the past. She tells me that a friend of hers is on the Lipotrim[©4] diet and asks me if it is safe for her to try it. In order to give informed advice I should be fully acquainted with the Lipotrim[©] diet. If I'm not, I can only answer that I don't know enough about the pros and cons of going on such a diet. Alternatively I can look up the Lipotrim[©] diet on the internet[5] and give an informed opinion to this lady, bearing in mind that such a diet cannot be suitable for everyone who wishes to lose weight gained as a result of years of binge-eating. The consultation becomes a dilemma. As soon as the lady leaves the consultation she is free to undertake whatever diet she chooses – the GP does not have ultimate control. The autonomy of the individual is respected.

I mention the Lipotrim[©] diet only as an example. Over the years there have been a myriad such diets on the market. I have had to familiarise myself with these diets and give informed advice to individuals. Many of them are household names – we've had the low-carbohydrate, high-protein Atkin's[©]diet[6] and the Nutron[©] diet[7], which claims to identify food intolerances by means of a blood test and devises a diet plan on that basis.

SCENARIO 2

A man in his late thirties attends for consultation, complaining of a back injury received at work. He is an infrequent attender at my practice. I address his concerns about his back injury, examine him and with his co-operation draw up a plan for the investigation and treatment of his back condition. I also use this consultation as an opportunity to measure his blood pressure – this is referred to as opportunistic health screening. I note that his blood pressure is elevated – yes, he has high blood pressure. I then proceed to measure his BMI, which is 31. I inform him that there are several issues which need to be addressed in addition to his back injury. Firstly, I will need to investigate and monitor his blood pressure. Secondly, I gently inform him that he is overweight (obese, in actual fact, but I do not want to compound a person's weight problem by using the term obese: the word 'overweight' is less stigmatising – unless they ask me directly if they are obese).

Then a sequence of proposals is put in motion. I encourage the patient initially by informing him that if he loses weight slowly over the coming months by reducing his caloric intake and taking regular exercise, his body weight will normalise and his blood pressure will probably go back to being normal. I also tell him that he is much more likely to lose weight if he attends a structured weight-reduction programme such as WeightWatchers[8]. Carrying less weight he will be less likely to re-injure his back and by keeping his weight under control he will be less likely to develop weight-related illnesses such as diabetes, heart disease and osteoarthritis in the future.

SCENARIO 3

A lady in her late forties attends for a well-woman check. This includes a full examination, urine and blood tests, breast screening, cervical smear and health and lifestyle advice. It is noted that her BMI is 35. When asked, she admits to having tried dozens of diets but with no success. She also admits that she is tired all the time, teary for no apparent reason and doesn't get out much. This is pretty much a classic picture of the overweight binge eater. It is estimated that 50 per cent of binge eaters are depressed – distressed by being overweight and unable to conquer it. This lady's mental wellbeing must be carefully evaluated and her symptoms of depression need to be addressed and treated in parallel with her eating disorder. So what starts as a pretty innocent health check evolves into a complex set of issues which need to be addressed, managed and treated appropriately.

From these three scenarios alone there are huge implications for the workload of the GP and the practice nurse, as well as for the Department of Health and Children and the government. Overweight and obese people are the product of BED or compulsive overeating[9], which is characterised as an 'addiction' to food, using food and eating as a way to hide from the emotions, to fill a void and to cope with daily stresses and problems .

TYPE 2 DIABETES

The most obvious consequence that has been observed in Ireland of people overeating for whatever reason is the epidemic of Type 2 diabetes[10]. It is estimated that 4.7 per cent of the population (200,000) have diabetes – 90-95 per cent of whom have Type 2 diabetes[11], previously known as 'non insulin-dependent diabetes mellitus' (NIDDM) or 'adult-onset diabetes.' People with Type 2 diabetes do produce insulin, but either they do not make enough of it or their bodies do not use the insulin they make to good effect. Most of the people who have this type of diabetes arc ovcrwcight, зо thcy may be able to control their condition by losing weight through diet and exercise. As well as following a healthy programme of diet and exercise, they may also need to inject insulin or take medicine. Although Type 2 diabetes commonly occurs in adults, an increasing number of children and adolescents who are overweight are also developing this condition. This is very worrying. It occurs because our children are overeating the wrong foods, drinking too many fizzy drinks, playing too many computer games and not exercising. Children with Type 2 diabetes do not typically present to the GP with the classic symptoms of adults with Type 2 diabetes but instead are diagnosed with the condition when they have a blood test or urine test for some other reason.

This development is a nightmare for economists, health-planners and the government. The increase in revenue required year on year to treat all these people newly diagnosed with Type 2 diabetes – all as a consequence of overeating – will run into countless millions of Euro. On a global scale, in 2000 the prevalence of diabetes for all age-groups worldwide was estimated to be 2.8 per cent and it is predicted to be 4.4 per cent in 2030. The total number of people with diabetes is therefore projected to rise from 171 million in 2000 to 366 million in 2030.[12]

DRUG TREATMENTS

What drug treatments are available in general practice to assist people in losing weight? Writing a prescription or taking a tablet is easy but what makes the difference is giving support to the person who needs to be motivated in the first instance and who needs make a permanent change in their lifestyle.

In the past, appetite suppressants were licensed for pre-scription. The drugs that were available on prescription mimicked amphetamines (anorexigenic brain stimulants, for example fenfluramine and phentermine) and were highly addictive so their licences were withdrawn in Ireland.

More recently four different drugs have been prescribed by GPs to help people who suffer from binge-eating and compulsive eating to lose weight.

The first is called orlistat[13] and is marketed under the trade name Xenical© by Roche. It is designed to treat obesity and its primary function is preventing the absorption of fats from the human diet, thereby reducing caloric intake. It is intended for use in conjunction with a GP-supervised reduced-calorie diet.

Unlike orlistat, which acts peripherally, sibutramine[14], marketed by Abbott as Reductil, is a centrally acting (that is, it acts in the brain) stimulant, chemically related to amphetamines. Its effect is to reduce a person's appetite, thereby reducing the amount the person eats.

The newest drug in the GP armoury is Rimonabant[15], marketed in Ireland as Acomplia©. It is an oral selective cannabinoid CB1 receptor antagonist. It is licensed for use as a weight-loss aid in obese or overweight patients with type 2 diabetes or dyslipidaemia (patients with hypertriglyceridemia and/or low serum HDL-cholesterol [the so-called good cholesterol] concentration). Rimonabant, taken for up to two years in conjunction with diet and exercise, produces greater weight loss than the placebo, although most of the weight loss occurs in the first year. Patients will need to be motivated to stick to a calorie-controlled diet and exercise plan to see the best results.

The manufacturers of the drug Sanofi-Aventis© have stated that the initial target group is patients with abdominal obesity plus an additional risk factor such as type 2 diabetes or dyslipidaemia (abnormality in, or abnormal amounts of, lipids and lipoproteins in the blood).

SYNDROME X – METABOLIC SYNDROME

The metabolic syndrome is also known as the insulin resistance syndrome, dysmetabolic syndrome and syndrome X. There is no precise definition of this syndrome but it represents a specific body phenotype in conjunction with a group of metabolic abnormalities that are risk factors for coronary heart disease (CHD). Characteristics of this syndrome include abdominal obesity, insulin-resistant glucose metabolism (hyperinsulinemia, high fasting plasma glucose concentrations, impaired glucose tolerance), dyslipidemia and hypertension.[16]

ABDOMINAL OBESITY[17]

Previously, most obesity experts considered that total body fat (as roughly estimated by measuring the BMI) was the main predictor of weight-related disease: the higher the body fat percentage, the higher the health risk. Now it is thought that location of fatty tissue is as important, if not more important, than total body fat.

Fat stored around the abdomen and waist is believed to be a better predictor of weight-related diseases like cardiovascular disease (CVD). Cardiovascular disease is the clinical result of atherosclerosis (narrowing of the arteries), and may lead to myocardial infarction (heart attack) or stroke. Intra-abdominal fat (IAF) is also associated with increased risk of hormonal cancers such as breast cancer, ovulatory dysfunction and obstructive sleep apnoea.

Your waist size can be an important measure of health.[18] Waist circumference is an indirect indicator of intra-abdominal fat tissue, often called visceral fat. A high waist circumference is associated with an increased risk of Type 2 diabetes, high cholesterol, high blood pressure, and cardiovascular disease because of excess abdominal fat. To measure your waist circumference, place a tape measure around your body at the level of the uppermost part of your hip bone (usually at the level of your navel). You are at increased risk of health problems if you are a man with a waist circumference greater than 102cm and if you are a woman with a waist circumference greater than 89cm.

GP EXERCISE REFERRAL PROGRAMME

In 2001 an initiative began in general practices in Cork which saw patients being prescribed exercise by their GPs. The 'GP Exercise Referral Programme'[19] aimed to provide a safe way for people with various health problems, including eating disorders, to become more active. Patients who, in the opinion of a GP, would benefit from regular exercise, were referred to a participating leisure centre. Prior to the national launch, the programme was successfully piloted in Cork for one year. An evaluation report of the pilot phase found that more than 120 people had been referred to the programme in 2001. The ages of participants ranged from twenty-two to eighty-four years, with the average age being fifty-four. Twice as many women as men took part, with home-makers making up the biggest number of referrals (35 per cent), followed by professionals (18 per cent) and retired people (14 per cent). The most common reason for referral was weight reduction. Other causes included high blood pressure, osteoarthritis and high cholesterol levels. Almost 80 per cent of participants completed the programme and continued to sustain the level of activity one month later.

The programme, which has now been rolled out nationally, is a partnership scheme between the HSE's health promotion department, the Irish College of General Practitioners and specified leisure centres nationwide.

ANOREXIA NERVOSA

'Anorexia nervosa is characterised by a relentless pursuit of thinness, a morbid fear of obesity, a refusal to maintain a minimally normal body weight, and, in women, amenorrhoea.'[20] Fortunately, anorexia is rare in general practice but when it does present itself it poses a formidable challenge to all concerned.

The classic case of the adolescent female who is underweight (defined as being 15 per cent or more under the weight than would be expected for a person of similar height) may present because her periods have stopped (amenorrhoea). On further enquiry, it may also emerge that this young lady is terrified of being fat. This is at the kernel of the problem. The young woman actually believea that she is fat and therefore has a distorted body image. Patients with anorexia are in complete denial. Anorexia may be rare and many so-called mild cases are never diagnosed, but in western society it is becoming more prevalent and is increasingly affecting males. The drive to achieve a clothes size of 'double zero' is fuelling the increase.

The treatment of anorexia is multi-disciplinary. It involves the sufferer, the family, the GP, referral to a psychologist for individual cognitive behavioural therapy (CBT) and – if there is concomitant psychiatric illness (for example, depression) – referral to a psychiatrist may also be necessary, as may treatment with antidepressant medication. There is no quick fix: the treatment may last months or years, and in the most severe cases, be lifelong. CBT is at the cornerstone of treatment.

Atypical (second generation) antipsychotics, for example Oanzapine, may help to relieve the morbid fear of obesity and may also help in producing weight gain. Once weight has been regained, Fluoxetine may be used to prevent relapse.

BULIMIA NERVOSA

Bulimia, although much more common than anorexia, is rarely a presenting problem in general practice. By its very nature, bulimia is a very secret affair, but unlike anorexia it is usually admitted to if the suffferer is listened to by a sympathetic ear. By definition bulimia nervosa consists of recurrent episodes of binge-eating (at least two per week for three consecutive months), followed by self-induced vomiting, laxative or diuretic abuse, vigorous exercise or fasting.[21]

Self-induced vomiting can cause destruction of the enamel on the front teeth by stomach acid, swollen salivary glands, scarring of the knuckles (caused by placing of the fingers down the throat to induce vomiting) and (rarely) may cause the oesophagus to tear and cause bleeding.

The treatment for bulimia is with cognitive behavioural therapy (CBT) and selective serotonin reuptake inhibitors (SSRIs), especially Fluoxetine. Bulimia nervosa afflicts 1 to 3 per cent of adolescent and young women. Those affected are persistently and overly concerned about body shape and weight. Unlike patients with anorexia nervosa, however, those with bulimia nervosa are usually of normal weight.

FEEDING DISORDERS AMONG NEWBORN BABIES

Feeding a newborn infant can post many problems for a mother, regardless of whether she is breast-feeding or bottle-feeding and GPs are faced with numerous questions, especially if the child is the first-born.

In our fast-moving maternity units, the newborn infant is often handed to its overwhelmed mother as if to say, 'Well done, you're the proud mother of a baby boy/girl. There you go.' It is as if the woman had been breast-feeding all her life and is expected to get on with it. Most new mothers feel unsure, insecure and guilty. What is vital is that a new mother be supported by somebody who can help her establish and maintain breast-feeding for as long as she wishes. In practice a woman may have problems with the baby not latching on properly to the nipple; she may have inverted nipples; she may develop mastitis. All these problems can be addressed and resolved with the right kind of support for the mother.

In the first couple of years of life babies are vulnerable to various infections, one of which is viral gastroenteritis or 'gastro', as it is commonly called. Babies may have vomiting or diarrhoea or both and the mother will present saying that the child is not feeding and cannot keep anything down. This is sometimes a dilemma, not because gastro is a serious illness in an infant, but because infants are prone to becoming dehydrated if vomiting and/or diarrhoea persists. If that occurs they have to be admitted to hospital for re-hydration and nursed in isolated units to prevent the spread of gastroenteritis to other patients.

After the child eliminates the gastro virus from the gastrointestinal tract, what frequently happens is that the enzymes in the gut responsible for digesting lactose (the sugar in milk) – lactases – become temporarily inefficient. The child may then develop lactose intolerance, whereby the gut cannot absorb any milk-containing food. This results in persistent diarrhoea. Fortunately this recovers of its own accord in a matter of days or a week or two and meanwhile the child is maintained on a lactose-free diet until fully recovered.

EATING PROBLEMS AMONG TODDLERS AND CHILDREN
There are many accounts of toddlers and young children going on 'hunger strike'. Let's look at a home with a toddler when a

new baby is brought home. Male or female – it doesn't matter – the toddler is jealous and wants to make a statement. She is too young to verbalise her emotions, so the only stick she has to beat her parents with is refusal, a very powerful weapon. The most common refusal is a refusal to eat or drink. This can cause consternation in a home with young children, adding to stress in an already very stressful household. The GP has to act to assuage the parents' fears that their 'hunger striker' will dehydrate or starve to death and reassure them that this is a normal human reaction to change. The problem has to be managed by the consensus of all those involved in the minding of the child – parents, babysitter, grandparents and child-minder. The approach is to be consistently fair but firm with the child – for example it would defeat the purpose if someone broke ranks and allowed the child treats and fizzy drinks between meals. The child's thirst and hunger will get the better of him/her and he/she will eventually agree to eat and drink normally at mealtimes like the other members of the family.

EATING PROBLEMS AMONG SCHOOLCHILDREN

Parents (usually mothers) often present for one reason and then mention that Johnny brings his lunch home from school uneaten every day. The child is not dehydrated or starving and appears to be getting by. How come? Here are some possible reasons. Johnny is feeling hungry at break-time and looks into his lunchbox and sees two bread rolls with cheese or ham, some pasta, an apple, an orange, a yoghurt, an Actimel and a bottle of water. Then his buddy Jack says, 'Hey Johnny – want a packet of Rolos?' What would you do if you were Johnny – you'd grab the Rolos and demolish them. Or it could be a bottle of Coke which again contains more than enough calories to satiate Johnny. His mother might also tell me that when she gives him his evening meal he only plays with it and won't eat it. What do I suggest is the cause?

Firstly, Johnny could be getting sweets, treats, crisps and fizzy drinks from another pupil or from the shop or from some other benefactor (such as a child-minder or a granny).

Secondly, if a child has a large drink of water, cordial, orange juice, yoghurt drink or fizzy drink (normal or diet) the mere volume of liquid will completely fill up their stomach (the first part of the gut) and they will feel full and have no space for food to go down. If they are forced to eat they may vomit the whole lot up. The rule is drinks in small amounts with food and/or drinks after food.

Thirdly, children can be stubborn and may refuse to eat in order to gain undivided attention and special time with a parent if they feel they are not getting it.

Older children (although this is increasingly affecting children at a younger and younger age) may be teased and bullied at school because they are overweight, and called names like 'fatso' and 'fatty'. This has a huge negative impact on the child's self-esteem and feelings of self-worth. It can lead to him or her not performing at school, refusing to go to school, feigning illness, requiring unnecessary visits to the GP, withdrawing from friends, withdrawing from sports, becoming reclusive, feeling depressed, having suicidal thoughts and even committing suicide. It is not just the bullied children who are affected; the whole family ends up in turmoil. Bullying is totally unacceptable under any circumstance and the GP's advice will always be to meet with the school principal and class teacher. It is my experience that bullying is more common amongst girls, and girls' bullying is more verbal than boys' physical bullying.

EATING DISORDERS AMONG THE ELDERLY

Eating problems are very common among the elderly. People are living into their eighties and nineties now and this poses an increasing challenge to all involved in the care of the elderly.

As we go through life our teeth suffer wear; we may lose some or all of our teeth. Some people will have partial dentures and others full denture plates. Also as we age, our lower jaw (mandible) starts receding, leading to chewing difficulties. These factors alone may determine the amount and types of food we eat. Such a change in diet can lead to vitamin deficiencies, protein deficiency, constipation and weight loss. This can have a knock-on effect on all the body systems, including the heart and brain.

In order to assess eating disorders in the elderly other factors must be taken into account. Take the logistics of an elderly lady in her eighties, living alone, suffering from poor vision and arthritis. How can we expect her to go to the supermarket, negotiate the week's shopping and cook hot food for herself every day, presuming that she can afford to. How can we guarantee proper nutrition for this lady? The answers are complex and involve the support of others, be they family, friends, neighbours or the local meals-on-wheels service.

General pracititioners often hear the expression 'taken to the bed'. This is never a good sign. A family will complain that their mother or father or relative has taken to the bed and will drink only tea. Such a development may be a symptom of a much more sinister underlying depressive illness, and comprehensive treatment of the depression will be required before the individual can regain a proper quality of life and eat and drink properly again.

Sometimes elderly people will not eat properly because they

are simply not hungry. It is true to say that as we grow older our appetite diminishes. However, appetite loss, especially in the elderly, can be a symptom of underlying cancer and this has to be investigated further. Appetite loss together with losing weight is an even more serious pointer towards underlying cancer in the elderly.

From time to time, the elderly person may not eat because 'it's too much trouble'. Think about it – you have aches and pains all over, your eyesight is not what it used to be, you get breathless or tired very easily – are you really going to prepare, cook and serve a full meal seven days a week every week of the year? Probably not. You may opt instead for a boiled egg or tea and toast, which is perfectly understandable. It may not make nutritional sense but it makes perfect common sense.

For the elderly, not eating properly may also be in response to some stress or trauma, such as becoming widowed, being hospitalised, feeling lonely or isolated, fearing dying alone or fearing death itself. All these issues have to be addressed and discussed with the patient. It doesn't matter if the fears are real or imaginary; they are impacting forcibly on an individual's daily life, their quality of life, their integrity and their very being. If I could write a prescription for loneliness I would be the most popular GP on the planet.

Many GPs in Ireland are attached to various institutions, from nursing homes to institutions for people with learning disabilities. In many instances the residents are full-time and the GP looks after their general health needs. Being in an institution implies that the residents are less active than those in the community. This sedentary lifestyle, coupled with their inability to take part in formal exercise programmes, is likely to lead to weight-gain. Most of the residents are on medication for their condition and some psychotropic medications (medications used to stabliise mood, mental status or behaviour) have weight gain as a side effect.

This poses serious problems for the GP in attempting to keep the residents healthy and preventing them from developing weight-related illnesses such as Type 2 diabetes, osteoarthritis, osteoporosis, chronic constipation and hypertension – to mention just some of the long list of medical diseases associated with being sedentary and overweight/obese. Some clients are confined to beds or wheelchairs so exercise isn't even an option. What is vital in such an institution is that the chef and the catering team realise the importance of healthy food served in the correct portions. This means that there has to be a consensus on the quantity and range of food served, the way foods are cooked (for example grilled, not fried) the salt, sugar and fat content, and a commitment to the reduction of foods high in cholesterol and processed foods.

SPORTING ACTIVITIES, SIZE AND WEIGHT
Dieting and the effort to be slim seem to pervade western society, making huge demands on men and women to conform to a standard. Some sporting activities add to this pressure.

In professional boxing there are different weight categories. If you weigh outside your category you cannot fight. Therefore you cannot work and earn a living. Boxers go to extremes to maintain their weight at a certain level. A GP may be asked to help a boxer to lose weight before a big fight, which may go against accepted evidence-based medicine. The same applies to horse-racing, where a jockey's weight is rigorously controlled.

Health and Safety legislation[22], implemented in line with EU directives, lays down that it is now mandatory to have medical professionals available for medical assistance at all sporting events.

In 1995 the Irish Rugby Union turned professional and a lot of children have become almost obsessed with rugby. Parents attending under-age matches and school cup matches will have noticed the massive increase in the size of boys who play rugby. The professional era has seen a reduction in the number of years a player normally plays, from ten to fifteen years down to half that. The reason is that the game has become very physical and high-impact. You can hear the thud of colliding schoolboys from the terraces during a match. This has implications for the general practitioner. There are very precise rules about returning to sport after sustaining concussion and a lot of pressure can be brought to bear on the team doctor, who is frequently a GP, to allow a key player back – but the rules on concussion are always applied and no exceptions are ever made.

When we look at rugby union footage from twenty or thirty years ago we see that most players were of average build. Even the All Blacks were, in general, fairly slim. But with the introduction of Western Samoan players into New Zealand the physical size of the All Blacks has become massive and this is what all other rugby nations around the world are aspiring to now. Size is such an issue in New Zealand under-age rugby that tournaments and matches are being limited to a specific age and the under-age groups are divided up according to weight so that small children are not injured by much heavier opponents.

Now Irish teenagers may come into the GP and asks if it's safe to take Creatine, a protein supplement used for muscle development. Although we all know of teenagers who take Creatine, it is not licensed for use by under-nineteens and cannot be recommended.

What GPs are facing, into the future, is an increasing demand for services to cope with the immediate and long-term consequences of over-eating, obesity, diabetes and all the complications of these conditions.

NOTES

1. *Merck Manual Professional.* http://www.merck.com/mmpe/sec15/ch199/ch199d.html>
2. Irish Health Promotion Unit. http://www.healthpromotion.ie/topics/obesity/>
3. Department of Health and Children. 'Obesity: the policy challenges'. http://www.dohc.ie/publications/report_taskforce_on_obesity.html>
4. http://www.lipotrim.demon.co.uk/>
5. http://www.lipotrim.demon.co.uk/master.htm>
6. http://atkins.com/
7. Information from the dietetics section of the VHI website. http://www.vhi.ie/experts/diet/diet_q174.jsp
8. WeightWatchers Ireland. http://find.weightwatchers.ie/
9. The Something Fishy Website on Eating Disorders. http://www.something-fishy.org/
10. The Institute of Public Health in Ireland'. 'Making Diabetes Count – What Does the Future Hold?' http://www.publichealth.ie/publications/makingdiabetescountwhatdoesthefuturehold
11. Weight-control Information Network (US). Glossary M thru Z http://win.niddk.nih.gov/publications/glossary/MthruZ.htm>
12. World Health Organization. http://www.who.int/diabetes/facts/en/diabcare0504.pdf

13. http://www.xenical.com
14. http://www.abbott.com/content/en_US/20.10.178:178/ product/Product_Master_0180.htm>
15. Acomplia: Information for Consumers and GPs. http:// www.acomplia.me.uk/
16. Obesity Online. http://www.obesityonline.org/slides/slide01. cfm?tk=42
17. http://www.anne-collins.com/articles/abdominal-obesity. htm
18. http://health.yahoo.com/experts/heartdisease/3586/waist-to-hip-ratio-vs-bmi-whats-the-better-heart-disease-predictor/
19. http://www.irishhealth.com/index.html?level=4per centamp;id=4321>
20. http://www.merck.com/mmpe/sec15/ch199/ch199b.html
21. http://www.merck.com/mmpe/sec15/ch199/ch199c.html
22. Health and Safety Legislation. http://www.hsa.ie

2

EATING DISORDERS: A PSYCHIATRIC PERSPECTIVE

AISLING CAMPBELL, CONSULTANT PSYCHIATRIST

This chapter will focus on anorexia nervosa and bulimia nervosa as these are the commonest eating disorders seen by the psychiatrist. Patients with simple obesity are rarely referred for psychiatric treatment. There are, of course, other forms of eating disorders such as non-specific eating disorders, binge-eating disorder, sub-threshold eating disorders (patients with some features but not the full clinical syndrome of anorexia and bulimia), many of which share some of the core psychopathology of anorexia and bulimia, and a wide variety of eating disorders of childhood. Of course, many eating disorders commence in the teens and some patients will attend a psychiatrist specialising in the assessment and treatment of adolescent patients. However, the general issues at stake and principles of treatment are much the same for teenagers as for adults although there may be subtle differences of focus. For the most part in this chapter, the female pronoun will be used for ease, although the incidence of eating disorders is increasing in males. The terms 'anorexic' or 'bulimic' may be used, again for ease, rather than in any attempt to objectify or label what is an individual person with significant psychological distress.

A common clinical scenario encountered by the psychiatrist is a young anorexic patient, usually female, brought to the consultation by a parent, usually although not always the mother. The patient can be spotted from a distance – very thin, she may be bundled up in baggy or warm clothes even in warm weather, and looks distinctly aggrieved at being in the psychiatric clinic. The psychiatrist asks the patient why she has been referred, or what she herself believes to be wrong, only to get monosyllabic or noncommittal answers. The patient, in fact, is quite satisfied with her life at present, and cannot understand what all the fuss is about! Despite the fact that she is grossly underweight, that her periods have stopped and that her parents cannot sleep at night because of worry, she feels perfectly well and in fact has plenty of energy. For the first time in her life she may feel in control – she has after all managed to diet successfully and may have been for a time the envy of her friends in this regard. She may even deny dieting, insisting that she eats normally, and may express surprise at her weight loss. Some patients will admit to dieting and may describe at some point realising or feeling that they were overweight. Many patients insist that although most people would look underweight at their weight, the normal rules do not apply to them and that they still look and are overweight. Whatever the pattern, there is usually huge resistance on the part of the patient to the prospect of increasing her food intake and she may react with horror to the suggestion that she needs dietetic advice.

The parent or parents then join the consultation – this may be with or without the patient present – and their anxiety is generally very clear. Indeed, there can be few other psychiatric disorders that generate so much anxiety on the part of parents, apart, perhaps, from drug dependency. Very often the anorexic can appear to be in control of the whole family, with everyone else frantically trying to ensure that she is eating enough. Parents often assume the worst and have many times rehearsed the 'worst-case scenario' in their own minds. Even after a few months of living with a child who is anorectic (or indeed bulimic) parents can get caught up in a cycle of anxiety and control with the anorexic, which rarely results in the anorexic getting better, but almost always causes significant stress for the parents.

The doctor will attempt to assess and diagnose the patient, decide whether or not there are other psychiatric disorders present, and will then decide on a treatment plan. Almost all patients with eating disorders can be treated as out-patients, and the best results come from a combined, team-based approach, involving psychiatrist, dietitian, psychologist and sometimes specific forms of therapy such as group therapy or family therapy. Many patients also benefit from attending a self-help group.

Some patients may require in-patient treatment at some point in their trajectory. The usual outcome is in fact fairly good – this is obviously a generalisation – although many patients have persistently abnormal eating attitudes for years after recovery. Recovery from an eating disorder is a slow process and it can take many years for a patient to move from needing to exert extreme control over food intake to being able to relax in, say, a restaurant, and eat what everyone else is eating. It is important for families to pace themselves for the long haul. Eating disorders in a family member tend to flush out family dynamics and therefore family members may find that they need to seek professional support for themselves.

Although the thumb-nail sketch painted above uses the example of anorexia, anyone living with a patient suffering from bulimia will recognise the anxiety that is also generated by this disorder. Indeed the clinical features of anorexia and bulimia are more similar than they are different and when discussing these disorders it is rarely helpful to get bogged down in the differences between them.

CLINICAL FEATURES OF ANOREXIA NERVOSA

No phrase sums up the clinical features of anorexia nervosa better the famous 'fear of fatness and pursuit of thinness' characterised by Hilde Bruch in her well-known book *The Golden Cage*. The anorectic really does 'pursue' thinness with passion, and this is her primary goal. Many patients describe always having felt fat, even as much younger children. However, patients may describe becoming aware of their weight in a fairly sudden fashion – for instance when they see photographs of themselves in a swim suit, or when being fitted for a bridesmaid's dress, or when friends start to diet. Sometimes their discomfort at their weight can be triggered by an ill-advised comment from a relative – 'She's a fine big girl' is a not-uncommon trigger. Others describe a sudden change in their perception of their visual image, often occurring around puberty.

For some patients, particularly girls, the onset of puberty is associated with many uncomfortable feelings, related to sexual identity and sexual attractiveness, and the eating disorder may well be an effective method of controlling and suppressing these feelings. However, the aetiology of eating disorders will be dealt with later in this chapter. An incident which underlines these sexual issues may act as a trigger for an eating disorder – it is not unusual to hear of a first sexual encounter or a sexual assault acting as a trigger.

Conversely, the eating disorder may not start with a conscious wish to lose weight at all – some patients describe losing weight through some other means, such as illness, or simply deciding to eat more healthily, and then finding that the weight loss continued. For these patients, it appears that they have serendipitously discovered weight loss as a way of increasing self-esteem, and then continue with this as a coping mechanism.

By the time an anorexic patient presents for treatment she is usually well-established in the core thinking pattern, or psychopathology, as described by Bruch. The need to lose weight and to continue to lose weight is paramount. The patient's thoughts are entirely focused on food and weight, and despite her success at dieting (often to the envy of her friends) she is never satisfied with her weight loss but strives to lose more. Self-esteem and mood are dictated by her food intake and weight. The patient will often assert that although others may look well at a normal weight, different rules apply to her. While others may look perfectly attractive with a normal body shape, her thighs look fat despite fitting well into the proverbial 'size zero' jeans.

Generally, the more weight the anorexic loses, the less satisfied she is with her weight and shape, so that the disorder becomes more entrenched with increased weight loss. This core thinking pattern is the key feature of anorexia nervosa and distinguishes anorexia from other causes of weight loss (for example depression, which may be associated with low self-esteem, and lack of interest in food but without the phobia about weight and primacy of thinness). Because the anorexic's life centres around weight and food, relationships tend to take second place. The anorexic's primary concern is the control of diet and weight on any given day – so others, particularly family members, may feel as though their own feelings are dictated by how pleased or otherwise the anorectic is with her pursuits. A less successful 'food day' (in which the anorexic has not restricted her intake as she would like) or a gain of a pound may result in significant distress, anxiety and tears, and everyone in the family suffers. The core psychopathology can be difficult to elicit in a clinical situation as many anorexics are masters of deception and may deny the presence of this core psychopathology. They may know very well what the features are, and that they have them, but in order to avoid having to gain weight, may claim that they would like nothing better than to gain weight. Denial, in other words, is a key feature of the disorder.

The word denial, however, does not fully capture the nature of the mental process involved. The patient knows very well, at some level, that they are suffering from a disorder and that their behaviour and obsessions are not normal. On the other hand, they need the disorder to continue in order to maintain a kind of mental balance or homeostasis and therefore cannot give up the disorder. As already noted, the eating disorder may be defending the person against more painful or intolerable feelings. To admit to having it would be to begin to abandon it. As the disorder becomes more chronic, anorectic thinking often becomes more entrenched and insight diminishes. The importance of a change in core thinking will be included in a discussion on treatment.

Distorted body image is a key feature of anorexia nervosa. Patients will insist that they look fat although they are plainly underweight or even cachectic. Like many aspects of anorexia nervosa, this distorted perception tends to worsen with increased weight loss. Some patients will focus particularly on the upper arms, thighs, abdomen and bottom areas and may spend hours scrutinising their reflection in the mirror, from all angles. Despite this, they have great difficulty in seeing how they look to others. Some writers have characterised this distorted body image as a delusion akin to the bizarre false beliefs sometimes seen in psychotic disorders such as schizophrenia. Although anorexia nervosa is not generally considered to be a psychosis, the distortion of body image can be so extreme as to be quasi-psychotic. But this symptom does not respond to medications used for the treatment of schizophrenia.

PHYSICAL FEATURES OF ANOREXIA NERVOSA

When does normal dieting become anorexia? Clearly, in order for a medical professional to make a diagnosis of anorexia nervosa, the core thinking pattern must be present. Usually once a patient presents (or is brought by a family member for treatment) she is obviously underweight. What about people who have just started to diet? Can they be diagnosed with anorexia at an early stage?

The answer is that in order for a diagnosis of anorexia nervosa to be made there must be a certain degree of weight loss. In the psychiatric classification systems that are used internationally, a weight loss of more than 15 per cent of the expected weight for height is required to make a diagnosis of anorexia nervosa. It appears that many patients have the core thinking pattern of anorexia nervosa before they reach this level of weight loss. However, the core thinking is usually not fully entrenched until weight loss reaches a significant level. Additionally, the expected weight for height is a range, not a single figure. For instance a person of 5' 6' might be of normal weight at anything between eight-and-a half and ten stone (112-147kg). Obviously if someone has started off at a weight of, say, ten-and-a-half stone, and has successfully dieted down to nine stone, they are not going to appear anorectic to their family. Some successful dieters manage to lose a reasonable amount of weight and stay at a more normal weight. Some will develop anorectic thinking – or may have started out with it – and will continue to lose weight and become more rigid in their anorectic thinking. Whatever the weight-loss trajectory, the anorexic will refuse to maintain a normal weight, or a weight above 85 per cent of the expected weight for height. The rate of weight loss may be gradual, may fluctuate, or in some case may be very rapid, particularly if the person has previously been very overweight. For the purposes of diagnosis, patients who have not lost 'enough' weight, as it were, to meet the criteria for anorexia nervosa, would be given a diagnosis of a non-specific eating disorder. Despite the difference in diagnostic label, the principles of treatment and recovery are the same.

Weight loss leads to a number of physical changes. The best-known of these is amenorrhoea, or the loss of menstruation. In fact, it is not at all unusual to find that the patient has stopped menstruating at a very early stage, after the loss of a few pounds, or even before any weight loss at all. The physiological or physical mechanism of the amenorrhoea is therefore not fully understood. It is clearly not directly related to weight loss but it is generally accepted that until the patient regains weight to a certain minimum weight (known as the 'critical weight'), menstruation will not return. Some patients may give a history of scanty periods or infrequent periods before the periods stop altogether. If anorexia nervosa begins before the girl has started to menstruate, the periods may be delayed (known as primary amenorrhoea – the loss of periods after menstruation has started is known as secondary amenorrhoea).

In my experience, many patients with anorexia nervosa are not particularly bothered by the loss of menses, despite its serious consequences in later life. With recovery and weight gain the periods usually return, albeit somewhat slowly. However, prolonged amenorrhoea can lead to osteopaenia (thinning of the bones) or osteoporosis (more serious thinning of the bones) and taking calcium supplements will usually not substitute adequately for the natural mechanism. Osteoporosis is a potentially painful condition which can lead in certain cases to fractures and to the collapse of spinal vertebrae. until the age of around thirty-five it can be reversed but obviously the more quickly the anorexic gains weight and resumes normal menstruation the better.

Blood tests to test the function of the ovaries (the female reproductive organs which produce eggs) can be done but are generally not useful in the management of anorexia nervosa. Obviously, the other major effect of amenorrhoea is infertility and this can become more of an issue later in life. Some patients may make a partial recovery through early adulthood or even into their thirties and may continue to have scanty periods, varying eating attitudes and slight underweight. These patients may require ovarian stimulation with hormonal treatment in order to conceive, but again, the ideal method of achieving fertility is through the resumption of normal eating and weight.

There is a number of other physical changes and complications that are associated with anorexia nervosa. Many patients feel the cold and may have cold, bluish fingers and toes, known as acrocyanosis. Often patients wear baggy clothing, either to conceal their weight loss or because they perceive themselves as overweight and unattractive. Some patients may develop a fine, downy hair, most commonly on the back and limbs This is known as lanugo hair and the cause of it is unknown. Patients who include carrots as a key part of their diet may develop an orange-hued discolouration of the skin, known as carotinaemia, caused by excessive intake of carotene, which is present in carrots.

Some patients develop dry skin.

Most people with anorexia nervosa appear to have boundless energy, often marching for miles in any weather, but at some point, fatigue becomes the norm, with increasing weight loss. Constipation, owing to low food volume, is common. Some patients who self-induce vomiting as a method of weight loss may develop calluses on the knuckles from sticking the fingers down the throat. Frequent vomiting may cause dental caries and occasionally swelling of the glands around the mouth area which produce saliva, giving the patient's face a slightly swollen appearance. Anaemia and vitamin deficiencies are rarer than might be expected but can occur.

The above physical signs are in themselves not hugely harmful. However, there can be more sinister consequences to ongoing starvation. While in the early stages of anorexia, weight loss is largely loss of fatty tissue, in later anorexia, muscle tissue may be broken down to provide fuel for metabolism, leading to muscle wasting. Some patients develop cardiac problems and cardiac arrest (the heart stopping) or other problems with heart rhythm can occur secondary to electrolyte imbalances in the blood. The commonest of these is low potassium. Potassium is an ion which is essential for the functioning of heart muscle and nerve tissue, and low potassium can result from repeated vomiting. Vomiting can also lead to a tear in the lining of the oesophagus, presumably due to the physical forces on the oesophagus involved in the vomiting of large volumes of food. Some patients who have restricted food intake for a long period may have a somewhat shrunken stomach; if these patients then re-feed suddenly on a normal diet, the stomach may swell suddenly and can impinge on the heart, which is nearby, causing heart rhythm problems. Hypothermia can occur as a result of chronically poor food intake. Very rarely, a patient may develop a brain syndrome secondary to malnutrition.

There is little doubt that anorexia nervosa can be associated with many potentially serious physical effects. The vast majority of these however, are reversible and most patients do not require in-patient treatment. However, physical complications may be an indication for in-patient treatment. Obviously the cardiac complications, in particular, are potentially dangerous, hence the importance of robust medical monitoring of patients with eating disorders.

BEHAVIOUR IN ANOREXIA NERVOSA

Anorexia nervosa is associated with a number of behaviours which families find upsetting. Most of these behaviours have one aim – to lose weight. The commonest method of weight loss by far is that of simple dietary restriction. The patient cuts out foods with a high fat and high carbohydrate content, and subsists on a low-fat, largely protein-based diet. The usual pattern is for the diet to become increasingly restrictive as time and weight loss progress. It is not uncommon to meet patients who manage to exist on a tub of low-fat cottage cheese and an apple per day! Many patients find it easier to restrict through breakfast and lunch as there are a large number of low-calorie options for those meals. Dinnertime is often more difficult. Patients often claim that they eat for dinner 'what everyone else is having' but further questioning reveals that their portion is a fraction of a normal one. Likewise, the butter, milk, yoghurt and so on that the patient claims they eat liberally will often turn out to the be the lowest fat types of these foods.

Arguments become a common feature of family mealtimes, with many families – particularly the cooks of the family – giving in to the patient's demands for only certain types of foods, or even allowing the patient to prepare her own meal separately from the family. Recipes are scrutinised rigorously by the patient; some patients may insist, for instance, on low-fat oil substitutes being used at all times, or on vegetarian food only. All of this makes for stressful family mealtimes.

Many patients count calories, although some focus more on fat and carbohydrate content. Inevitably the calorie content of the diet decreases as time progresses. A normal calorific requirement for a young woman could be as much as 2500 kilocalories (conventionally referred to as 'calories'). Patients with anorexia nervosa will usually be on less than 1000 calories and very many patients will be subsisting on far less – I have seen patients whose self-alloted intake is 200 or 300 calories per day.

Despite the dramatic restriction of diet, patients with anorexia are obsessed with food, hence the name 'anorexia', meaning loss of appetite, is a misnomer. In fact, appetite is usually only lost entirely with very extreme weight loss. Many anorexics dream about food and are quite obsessed with it by day. They may devour diet magazines and often display a fascination with what others are eating, even irritating friends and family by taking bits of food from their plates. Some anorexics will pick at food rather than sitting down to eat proper meals, shaving slivers off cakes and so on. Obsessional behaviours around meals may develop. It is not unusual to hear that the anorexic will only eat at 8 am, 1 pm and 6 pm for instance, with no deviation allowed. Some anorexics may cut their food up into a certain number of pieces and cannot tolerate eating unless this ritual is followed. Cutting food up into small pieces can be a strategy to avoid eating and many patients will simply push their food around the plate, making it appear that they have eating heartily when the opposite is true.

As families become increasingly concerned about the patient's weight loss, the patient develops better strategies to conceal the extent of her dietary restriction, so that deception and subterfuge become the norm. The anorexic may hide food in her napkin, making it appear that she has cleared her plate. Food may be disposed of in unlikely places, for instance in potted plants, and even in a supervised in-patient treatment setting I have seen food hidden under mattresses, in ventilation shafts and even thrown out of a window. Some anorexics hoard food, with no intention of eating it, and then conceal it in their bedroom, where it rots away and is eventually discovered by other family members.

Excessive exercise is an obvious method of weight loss and often becomes a central part of the anorexic's daily regime. The patient may stride up and down vigorously for miles, in cold, wet, snow or hail. Many anorexics welcome bad weather in the belief that weight loss will be greater if they have to produce body heat against the elements. Patients who favour exercise as a weight-loss method may feel very anxious and agitated if they cannot exercise or if they are prevented from doing so. It is not unusual to find that patients who are officially on bed-rest as part of a treatment regime have been exercising furiously under the covers.

Self-induced vomiting may also be used as a method of weight loss although it is more traditionally associated with bulimia and therefore will be described under that heading.

Some patients take large quantities of laxatives, although the effect of these tends to be more fluid loss than fat loss. Laxatives in very large quantities may reduce the absorption of food through the gut. Some patients also use excessive quantities of diuretics but again, the result of these is fluid loss rather than fat loss (although significant fluid loss will register as weight loss on the scales). Chronic use of large amounts of diuretic can lead to low blood potassium levels which may cause heart rhythm problems, similar to those resulting from persistent vomiting. Most effective diuretics are available only on prescription although some herbal diuretics are available on the internet. The use of any medicine which alters fluid and electrolyte balance, without medical monitoring, is dangerous.

All anorexics are obsessed with thinness and this may manifest in other behaviours. Many weigh themselves at least daily and often several times a day. Weight changes of two lbs or more per day are the norm for the average person, but for the anorexic, a tiny difference in weight can make the difference between a 'good' day and a 'bad' day, with the mood altering accordingly. Some anorexics may focus more on caloric intake, or even on fat and carbohydrate content, or on body shape, rather than on weight as such; but most anorexics spend a considerable amount of time, often many hours, studying their body in the mirror (mirror-gazing). They will usually focus on particular areas of the body, notably the abdomen, buttocks, upper arms and thighs, as these are the fattiest areas of the body and the areas which most change shape at puberty.

Despite her extreme thinness, the anorexic sees herself as fat rather than thin. This distorted body image, a characteristic feature of anorexia, is particularly frustrating for families as it is so difficult to understand how someone so visibly underweight believes that she is overweight. This distorted body image may be exacerbated by mirror gazing. It is as though the anorexic cannot see her body as a whole, as others see it, but rather as different parts which are focused on separately, none of which is satisfactory. The anorexic may well assert that although she herself may be a size 4 or 6 (or size 'zero' to use the parlance of popular television), others look slimmer than she at size 12 or more. She may express envy of the (normal) slimness of others, while declaring herself disgusted at her own much slighter figure. The distortion of body image can be so pervasive and resistant to persuasion or reassurance by others that it can seem almost delusional. For many patients the achievement of a normal body image takes a long time to return fully, despite weight gain. Interestingly, distorted body image was not a feature of the early descriptions of anorexia nervosa (which date back to 1874) – those early anorexics were preoccupied with fasting but looking thin did not appear to be a central feature of their psychopathology. It is possible that our culture, which is a highly visual one, has shaped the presentation of anorexia, so that the focus of modern anorexics is on visual image, or body image.

OTHER PSYCHIATRIC SYMPTOMS

Anorexia can be associated with other forms of psychopathology, or psychological symptoms, which may not be directly related to food or weight. Obsessive-compulsive-type symptoms are common – these most usually involve rituals surrounding food preparation or eating, but may extend to involve other areas of the person's life. For instance, some patients ritualise food preparation, weighing every ingredient down to the last gramme, or may have to arrange food in a certain manner on the plate. Some anorexics may attempt to impose eating rituals on their families (the most usual example being the demand that meals are served 'on the dot') and this can cause considerable stress for the family, who often give in to these demands on the grounds that if they do not, the anorexic will not eat at all.

The general thinking style of many anorexics is obsessional, in the sense of being over-controlling or perfectionist – for example, the anorexic may believe that if they even look at food they will gain weight (an example of magical thinking). They may obsessively balance the energy 'books', down to the last calorie eaten versus that used in exercise, and ruminate on food and weight to the exclusion of all else. Some anorexics may develop cleaning rituals or checking behaviour (for example, checking several times that switches are turned off), although it is unusual to find the anorexic ruminating on any subject other than food or weight or related subjects.

Depressive symptoms are common among anorexics, although, in the earlier stages of anorexia, the patient may come across as almost euphoric (unlike her family who are usually very anxious). She has, after all, discovered something that she can control, perhaps at a time when little else in her life is under control, and it is not surprising that this brings a degree of satisfaction. As her weight loss has progressed, others may have congratulated her on her will-power, and have probably envied her. She therefore may be experiencing little in the way of mood symptoms. Some patients do become depressed, particularly at a later stage in their illness. This may be partially because life becomes increasingly restricted as the illness progresses, or it may be partly related to sheer starvation. While suicidal ideation is rare in the early or middle stages of anorexia – perhaps because weight loss and food restriction appear to offer a solution to painful emotions – it can occur in depressed patients and some patients do commit suicide. Anxiety symptoms are part and parcel of anorexia as the anorexic is constantly anxious about weight and food intake and indeed may use dietary restriction as a method – albeit not a particularly healthy one – of anxiety management.

CLINICAL FEATURES OF BULIMIA NERVOSA

There is considerable overlap between anorexia and bulimia in terms of clinical features. Indeed, 50 per cent of people with bulimia have had a history of anorexia. The core psychopathological beliefs – that control of weight and food intake is the ideal – are present in both groups. People with bulimia might be considered to be less successful at restricting than are anorexics. They fluctuate between a pattern of restriction and then of overeating or bingeing, and often use the other methods of weight loss as described above, as well as self-induced vomiting, which can be a significant and dangerous feature in many patients. Patients with bulimia, like the anorexic, wish to be thinner and thinner and generally attempt to restrict significantly in order to achieve this. At some point, however, control breaks down and they binge. Bingeing is usually associated with feelings of shame and frustration and is often dealt with by self-inducing vomiting (although not always – some patients simply respond to a binge by restricting more severely, or by exercising). Vomiting brings some relief, although a period of bingeing is inevitably followed by vows to restrict further and never to binge again. Unfortunately, the more rigid the self-imposed rules become, the more difficult it is for the bulimic to stick to them and therefore the more likely it is that she will binge.

Bulimic patients tend to have greater subjective distress than do anorexics and are more likely to be depressed and to self-harm. They do not have the severe body image distortion of the anorexic but instead have body image disparagement. They perceive the shape of their body reasonably accurately but have an intense dislike of it, or of particular body parts, usually those on which the anorexic also focuses. Unlike the anorexic the bulimic is of normal weight or is slightly overweight. Weight is probably the most useful objective feature in distinguishing diagnostically between anorexia and bulimia. Some anorectic patients also binge, and this has given rise to the rather clumsy title 'bulimarexia'. It is probably easiest to conceptualise the disorders as being part of a broad spectrum of eating disorders, with abnormal eating attitudes at their core.

Probably because of the subjective distress that is associated with bulimia, sufferers tend to be more motivated to seek help than is the case with anorexia. However, many people who binge feel a significant sense of shame about their behaviour and this may militate against their seeking professional help or family support. Some people conceal their behaviour because they want to lose weight and quite correctly fear that they will have to change their ways and abandon their quest for the ideal weight if they seek professional help. Families may notice the telltale signs of vomiting – the patient may always leave the table immediately after eating (to go to the bathroom to vomit), or there may be evidence of vomit around the toilet. Some families have found that their indoor plants have been fertilised with a substantial dose of vomit. Simultaneously, the fridge and kitchen cupboards may be rapidly denuded of food and occasionally one hears of families who have had to lock up their food to prevent a week's groceries being consumed in a binge.

As already noted, a large proportion of people who develop bulimia nervosa have a history of anorexia nervosa. The anorexic who previously managed to maintain a restricted diet may either be unable to sustain this any longer because of hunger or the displeasure associated with restriction. Eating food that is not already on the 'safe' self-prescribed regimen may then be perceived by the anorexic as bad – while some people will respond to this idea by restricting further or exercising, some seem to be unable to control the urge to eat more and will binge. This can lead in some instances to progression to bulimia and it is rare in these circumstances for the patient to regain their anorexic control and return to restricting only. However, in some patients bulimia is the pattern from the start. Bulimia most commonly presents in a slightly older age group than anorexia. It may be that it is easier to be anorectic when younger as most young teenagers do not have significant choices in terms of diet, or do not have the access to food that bulimia requires. For older patients living independently, bingeing is easier as a greater range of foods is accessible.

Binges usually consist of large quantities of 'forbidden' foods, in other words, foods with a high fat, sugar or carbohydrate content that the bulimic would normally not allow themselves in the context of a restricted, low-energy diet. Many bulimics comment that they know that they will binge on a particular day as soon as they wake. Some describe the period before a binge as being 'on auto-pilot' as though they are detached from rational thinking. For those involved in treating people with bulimia, it is important to establish whether what the bulimic describes as a binge is in fact a binge or not. Some patients who have chronically restricted will have a very inaccurate sense of a normal meal and may describe as a binge what most people would consider a light meal. Notwithstanding this caveat, however, binges usually consist of large quantities of food which are eaten in private and often in haste, and almost never with any enjoyment. Large amounts of fluid may be consumed with the food in order to assist vomiting afterwards.

Binges may occur relatively sporadically or up to several times a day and can be time-consuming. Bingeing is associated with marked feelings of self-disgust and guilt; some of this is relieved by vomiting. The bulimic may be exhausted afterwards and may even sleep. Many patients comment that they are more likely to binge in the evenings, perhaps because they are unoccupied, bored, lonely, tired or may find it easier to justify a binge after a hard day's work or study.

Binges may occur for no obvious reason or may be triggered by feelings of sadness, anxiety, anger, guilt or by external events such as perceived rejection by others. Whether or not sleep intervenes, the aftermath of the binge is associated with significant guilt, and with vows to make up for the calorific content of the binge by restricting further or using other methods of weight control. It is as though the bulimic is always trying to 'balance the books' in terms of energy intake – and she always considers herself to be 'in the red', to extend the metaphor.

The thinking patterns that are associated with this pattern of bingeing followed by vomiting and/or restricting are character-istic of bulimia and tend to perpetuate the disorder. The bulimic defines herself and her self-worth in terms of whether or not she has managed to stick to a restricted diet. If she has not, she has been 'bad' and must compensate for it. A 'good' day would be one in which she has managed to stick to the diet. Obviously this type of black-and-white thinking tends to have effects on self-esteem. The bulimic sets herself increasingly rigid rules by which to live and eat and in a sense is setting herself up to fail. This sense of having failed yet again to live by these rigid rules leads to depressed mood and low self-esteem. Despite the consequences, the bulimic, like the anorexic, clings to the belief that if only she could get down to some magical weight – always less than her current weight – she would be able to feel well and live normally. Unfortunately the price to be paid for achieving a lower weight is that the disorder – and this is true of both anorexia and bulimia – gets a firmer grip on the individual. For the various reasons outlined, both disorders are self-perpetuating.

Self-harming behaviour is seen more commonly in bulimia than in anorexia. This may be partly because of the greater sense of subjective distress experienced by the bulimic. In some cases one has the sense that self-harming – for example, cutting – serves a similar purpose to bingeing. Some patients describe a sense of relief and release from cutting that is similar to the effect of vomiting after a binge. Both anorexia and bulimia are associated with a risk of suicide and it is thought that suicide is the leading cause of death in anorexia. The statistics for suicide in bulimia are inconclusive but it can occur and the risk should be considered carefully.

PHYSICAL EFFECTS OF BULIMIA

While amenorrhoea – loss of menstruation – is one of the signs of anorexia, in bulimia the periods may be irregular, scanty or normal. Otherwise the physical effects and risks associated with bulimia are similar to those associated with anorexia, without the cachexia (extreme thinness), acrocyanosis (bluish fingers and toes), lanugo hair and muscle wasting. The risk of low blood potassium levels is significant in patients who vomit frequently and this can be associated with heart rhythm abnormalities. Repeated vomiting can also give rise to erosion of the dental enamel and dental caries. The presence of stomach acid in the mouth may contribute to swollen parotid (salivary) glands on each side of the cheeks which may cause the bulimic person to have a rather 'chubby cheeks' appearance. The physical effort of vomiting may cause tears of the lining of the oesophagus. The occasional patient has calluses on some of the knuckles of either hand, a result of the knuckles repeatedly rubbing against teeth when fingers are used to self-induce vomiting. Obviously, some patients may smell of vomit shortly after vomiting, despite the use of mouth wash and other strategies to conceal their behaviour.

OTHER PSYCHIATRIC SYMPTOMS

Depressed mood is common in the context of bulimia and may merit treatment in its own right. Anxiety symptoms may also occur, as can obsessional symptoms such as cleaning and checking, although these are less common than in anorexia. Some patients with bulimia may also abuse alcohol or drugs (both of which may act as triggers for a binge) and a constellation of behaviours including bulimia, substance misuse, self-harming, sexual promiscuity and serious interpersonal relationship difficulties may suggest a more serious underlying personality problem which will not be solved by treatment of the eating disorder alone. Patients with bulimia who are also abusing substances are less likely to respond to treatment as substance misuse can act as a trigger for bingeing.

EATING DISORDERS IN MEN

While eating disorders are less frequent in men, the pattern is changing to a degree and male anorexics and, more rarely, bulimics are presenting for treatment. It is likely that there are many other men with eating disorders who are not seeking treatment, and stigma is probably one of the reasons for this state of affairs. While obviously the diagnostic criterion of amenorrhoea for anorexia nervosa does not apply to men, the majority of men (and women) with the disorder will have reduced libido.

The generally accepted wisdom, based on experience, was that males with eating disorders had more abnormal thinking and tended to be more difficult to treat than females. This appears to be changing to a degree in that one now sees more males with typical anorectic pathology. Bulimia in males is still rare outside of specialised clinical settings but it is likely that the incidence is increasing. Many authors on the subject have suggested that excessive exercising or exercise addiction in men may represent a gender-determined form of anorexia in men. In general, men with either exercise addiction or eating disorders are rarely seen by psychiatrists outside of very specialised eating disorder treatment centres and therefore it is difficult to generalise.

AETIOLOGY

The word 'aetiology' means the origins of a disorder. The word causation is rarely used in psychiatry or even in medicine in general as it implies the existence of a single causative agent, in the manner of, say, the E. Coli bacterium causing gastroenteritis. Obviously, in mental disorders things are not that simple and aetiology – which suggests multiple factors contributing to a disorder – is the preferred terminology. There is no doubt that eating disorders are multifactorial in origin and these factors will be examined below.

SOCIOLOGICAL FACTORS

Much is made of the fact that Western culture in particular emphasises visual image and appearance above the other characteristics of an individual. There is no doubt that teenage girls, in particular, respond to perceived external pressures (no matter how much they may protest their wish to be individual) and the preferred body shape is still that of slimness or even thinness. Moral value can be attached to this ideal body shape.

The predominant cultural discourse is to bemoan consumerism, and covert messages from many sources (not only the much-maligned media) suggest that over-consumption of food and other resources is morally wrong. There is admiration for people who have the ability to do without, to eat less or more healthily, to buy nothing, to reject labels, and so on. By the same token, people who are obese – while undoubtedly at greater and very real risk of a variety of diseases – are often perceived as lacking in moral fibre.

Human nature is such that we are never completely in tune with our appetites (unlike animals) and therefore someone who controls their appetite effectively may be seen as having strengths that the rest of us lack. Eating disorders at one time were rare in non-western cultures but as other cultures have become increasingly Westernised, the incidence (or rate of occurrence) of eating disorders has risen accordingly in those cultures.

Japan is a good example of a culture that has become increasingly influenced by Western ideals and where rates of eating disorders have been rising in recent years. Likewise, it has been shown that as the average waistline measurements of *Vogue* models has decreased (since the 1950s), eating disorders have become more common. While some of this increase may simply be due to people seeking professional help more often, it is likely that there has been a real rise in eating disorders.

However, it is perhaps simplistic to blame the visual media for the rise in eating disorders. What is more probable is that cultural influences may shape the form of the disorder but that if societal expectations were different, people would develop different symptoms. As has already been noted, while historical descriptions of anorexia do not include the distorted body image considered so typical nowadays, the other symptoms in these early descriptions are typical of present-day anorexics.

PSYCHOLOGICAL FACTORS

Psychological factors in the aetiology of eating disorders merit an entire book in themselves and will therefore only be summarised here. The comments that follow are based on clinical experience rather than on formal research. While there does not appear to be a clear personality type that is associated with anorexia nervosa, or bulimia nervosa, some personality characteristics do occur frequently. Many patients are overly sensitive to the opinions of others. Low self-esteem is almost inevitable, and many are unassertive in the context of relationships, being more tuned in to the needs of others than to their own needs. Guilt and the need to make recompense tend to motivate much of their behaviour. Perfectionism and a tendency to suppress emotions are common. Many people with eating disorders are not adept at identifying their own emotions and naming them. It can be helpful, in treatment, for the patient to keep a diary documenting eating patterns vis-à-vis emotions – many bulimic patients in particular are not good at recognising emotional triggers for binges. Some patients do have a history of obesity in childhood or in the early teens. However, some report having always felt dissatisfied with their body although they may have been of normal weight. This sense of having almost taken up too much space may have been present for some time or can dawn on the individual very suddenly.

Some workers in the area of eating disorders assert that these disorders have little, in fact, to do with food in psychological reality. However, it cannot be denied that food always carries an emotional charge at some unconscious level. For the baby, eating is one of the very first interactions with parents – feeding, after all, is the focus of much of the baby's early life and in a sense can represent both the giving and taking of love, and the struggle for independence and identity. As children grow and become more independent, the emotional charge surrounding food becomes suppressed to an extent (although most parents remain concerned with what and how their children eat at any age). In adolescence, there is again a drive for independence and identity – and at the same time the adolescent is still emotionally dependent on parents – and food and weight can become the arena in which this struggle is played out again. It is as though the primitive dynamics within a family – particularly between a child and parents – become dredged up again in the teens, and food can represent these dynamics to a certain extent.

For most children, appetite and food are taken for granted – most children may not even be aware of being hungry until they are called to the table for a meal. However, at some point this 'age of innocence' stops and food becomes more emotionally charged. Some patients describe becoming suddenly aware of their body – often around puberty or at some landmark occasion on which physical appearance is called into question. For some, it may be seeing themselves in a holiday photograph, or even at the first communion or confirmation stage, or their first time as a bridesmaid. Suddenly the body is no longer neutral – it is as though the body is seen for the first time by its owner as others may see it, . Some patients do not necessarily start to diet purposely but may lose weight for some other reason – physical illness for instance – and then start to experience the rewards inherent in weight loss and weight control.

The need to be in control is a common theme among people with eating disorders, and eating disorders could be seen as one possible choice made by an individual who at some point in their lives needs to establish control. It is a truism that adolescence is a time of emotional turmoil, involving separation from family and identification with peers in order to establish identity. In the 1950s, psychiatrists and psychologists unfairly blamed mothers for many problems. However, clinical experience does suggest that eating disorders may represent an attempt to push away the parents, particularly the mother, in order to establish a sense of separate identity. It is possible that food and eating symbolise the early emotional interaction between child and mother, or child and primary carers.

While it is not possible to generalise, sexual issues are also important for many patients with eating disorders. While by no means all patients with eating disorders give a history of sexual abuse, a proportion do, although the statistics vary from study to study. There is no evidence whatsoever that sexual abuse 'causes' eating disorders and one very large study showed in fact that sexual abuse may be associated generally with a very wide range of psychiatric disorders. Many patients with eating disorders have never been sexually abused. It is probably closer to the truth to say that sexual issues of all types become more urgent at adolescence. Whether it is sexual abuse, or normal infantile sexual feelings that have been buried in older childhood, adolescence brings these issues to the fore again. Some people respond by developing an eating disorder.

A number of writers in the field have suggested that anorexia represents an attempt to prevent the development of the sexual characteristics of the body. There is no doubt that the size of breasts, hips and so on is limited by starvation and many anorexics avoid relationships with the opposite sex. Some people with bulimia may engage in chaotic and sometimes promiscuous sexual relationships which mask significant problems with emotional intimacy. Sometimes a first sexual encounter or even a sexual assault can act as a trigger for the onset of an eating disorder. Of course, not all eating disorders have an onset in adolescence – some come on earlier, some much later – and it is likely that multiple factors determine the time of onset, depending on the current life issues for the individual.

Since the publication of the research of family therapist Salvador Minuchin and others in this area, there has been much interest in family dynamics and eating disorders. Professionals who use a family-based approach to understanding and treating eating disorders think of the family as a system in its own right. Like all systems, the family unit is always trying to achieve a kind of balance of energies, known as homeostasis. The person with an eating disorder within the family may at some level be trying to bring about homeostasis again after a change, or to control some dynamic within the family. Sometimes the eating disorder may solve a problem within a family, or keep the focus away from another problem. For example, a teenager may develop an eating disorder after the parents announce that they are separating – the eating disorder then becomes the focus of attention and may defer the separation.

The role of eating disorders in family dynamics tends to be more obvious in younger patients and there is good evidence from research that family psychotherapy is more useful than individual psychotherapy in patients with anorexia nervosa who are under eighteen. Those who are over eighteen tend to do better with individual therapy. Whether or not a clear role for the eating disorder in resolving family conflicts can be seen, eating disorders tend to change family dynamics and these changes can perpetuate the disorder. This will be discussed further under the heading of treatment.

PHYSICAL FACTORS

There is no clear underlying physical cause for eating disorders and the hormonal changes that are associated with anorexia in particular are almost certainly secondary to the disorder itself. There has been some research looking at brain neurotransmitters (the chemicals responsible for the functioning of brain cells) but although depression and obsessive compulsive symptoms may be associated with particular brain chemistry changes, no clear-cut underlying brain pathophysiological changes have been identified in anorexia or bulimia.

There is some evidence that genetics may play a role in the development of eating disorders. Certainly, it is not uncommon to find that a patient with anorexia nervosa or bulimia nervosa has a mother, sister, cousin or aunt with the disorder. It is still unclear as to whether this finding is related to having genetics in common, inherited personality traits, or an environment in common.

PERPETUATING FACTORS

Most of what has already been discussed under the heading of aetiology could be described as either vulnerability factors or triggering factors. However, many aspects of eating disorders in themselves perpetuate the disorder. Many of us admire those who have the willpower to lose weight and this attitude may subtly perpetuate the eating disorder. For instance, a schoolgirl may gain the admiration and envy of her friends if she alone successfully loses weight and it may be difficult for her to give up this new-found status. For many anorexics, the internal satisfaction of being in control of some aspect of their lives can be its own reward. Some patients describe a feeling of (almost) elation in the context of starvation and may experience increased awareness and intensity of perceptions – colours appear brighter, sounds louder – which may act as a perpetuating factor.

The denial that is so often associated with anorexia in particular tends to perpetuate and 'feed' the disorder – the more weight the anorexic loses, the more rigid her denial becomes. The anorexic's focus is so exclusively on food and weight that it is almost impossible for her to see the anxiety that it provokes in her family. Obviously if the eating disorder is serving some purpose within family dynamics, it is very difficult for the sufferer to abandon it. Sometimes family members – particularly parents – may take up a position of being responsible for the patient's eating and this can have the effect of removing the responsibility from the patient. While at times this may be necessary, it may prevent the patient from feeling the full effects of the eating disorder and thus may perpetuate it. While bulimia tends to be associated with less internal satisfaction than anorexia, the black-and-white thinking that is associated with the cycle of bingeing and vomiting tends to lead to further bingeing and vomiting, as already described.

AETIOLOGY – SUMMARY

To summarise: the aetiology of eating disorders is complex and it is likely that multiple causative factors operate in individual patients. A useful model is to think of eating disorders as a way in which a person may choose to resolve conflicts and problems in their lives, this choice perhaps having been triggered by some personally meaningful event. These conflicts may be external ones, relating to family and other environment; and internal ones, related to their own psychological make-up. Personality traits or qualities may play a role in determining whether or not someone develops an eating disorder, or deals with their problems in other ways. Many aspects of the eating disorder itself act as perpetuating factors. Some features of eating disorders may be influenced by societal values and the media.

TREATMENT

As with many mental disorders, the treatment of eating disorders is not a simple matter. Much depends on the patient's own motivation, which may fluctuate between good and non-existent. A purely medical model of treatment, with treatment administered by a doctor to a compliant patient, is not applicable in this situation. Even with the best motivation in the world, abnormal eating attitudes take a considerable amount of time to adjust. Patients and families must change – and mental changes cannot be hurried. However, on a positive note, the outcome for the vast majority of patients with eating disorders is good. A small proportion have a very poor outcome – and there are, tragically, a small number of patients who die of their eating disorder – and a percentage have a moderate outcome.

MOTIVATION AND TREATMENT OF ANOREXIA NERVOSA

Most patients with anorexia nervosa are at best ambivalent about recovery. Many do not want treatment at all and if left to their own devices would happily remain anorectic, despite the health risks and limited quality of life associated with the disorder. Very many anorexics are brought to treatment at the behest of family members who are almost always far more concerned about the anorexic than she is about herself. While the anorexic usually knows right well that she has the disorder, she is almost always ambivalent about weight gain, which is a sine qua non of any effective treatment programme.

Many anorexics come to treatment, giving the appearance

of compliance, but vowing privately that they will go along with anything as long as they do not gain weight. Although an addiction model alone cannot be applied to all aspects of the disorder, in this respect anorexia has much in common with alcohol or drug addiction. It is only when the suffering associated with the disorder is greater than the suffering associated with recovery that the anorexic will start to consider real participation in treatment. Additionally, changes within the family dynamics are almost always necessary for the anorexic to take on some of the responsibility for her own recovery.

One of the roles of the psychiatrist is to try to motivate the patient into active participation in treatment. This is easier said than done. Education about the physical risks associated with chronic starvation, bingeing and purging may be part of the clinical interview. Some patients are genuinely scared by the prospect of osteoporosis, for example, although many are convinced that it will never happen to them. If the anorexic is already experiencing physical discomfort – for example, fatigue – then education about long-term physical risks may be well-timed.

The psychiatric assessment will also focus on the person's mental state and the degree of psychological distress they are experiencing. Anorexics are adept at suppressing painful emotions and may have difficulties in becoming aware of their emotions. An opportunity to discuss the painful reality of living with anorexia may allow the patient a chance to take a more objective view of his or her current life situation. In reality, however, some external leverage is necessary to motivate the anorexic to treatment. She may be so fatigued that she is unable to continue school or third level studies. Although most anorexics continue with a surprising level of both physical and intellectual activity at a fairly low weight, concentration may be limited when the patient is preoccupied with food and weight. Many anorexics are high achievers so the loss of concentration may act as a motivator. Sometimes a sudden physical event such as a faint or collapse may act as a motivator. Employers or work colleagues will usually have noticed the patient's weight loss and may insist on treatment, usually after an incident such as a fainting spell at work.

THE MULTI-DISCIPLINARY TEAM AND TREATMENT OF ANOREXIA NERVOSA

The ideal management of anorexia nervosa and indeed bulimia nervosa is via a multi-disciplinary team approach. This means that a number of professional perspectives are brought to bear on the eating disorder, working as a team rather than as individuals. Clear communication between professionals on the team is essential as potentially the patient may well 'split' the team, in other words, play one off against the other. The potential for splitting is lower when the professionals involved have experience in treating patients with eating disorders. Parents and other carers of those with eating disorders will be only too familiar with splitting and it is not uncommon to find one parent portrayed by the anorexic as uncaring and the other idealised. As with the team, families need to be aware of this dynamic and avoid collusion with it. The professionals who may be involved in a team treating eating disorder patients might include the following:

- Psychiatrist
- General Practitioner
- Psychologist or psychotherapist

- Dietitian
-

and possibly:

- Nurse therapist or art therapist (instead of a psychologist or psychotherapist)
- Occupational therapist

While the other professionals writing in this book have outlined in greater detail their role, it is worth considering here the roles which each plays, and the possible overlap between them. The minimum team required for the majority of patients would be a general practitioner, dietitian and a psychiatrist. Regular psychological input is necessary for very many patients and this can be at least partially delivered by the psychiatrist, or more commonly by the psychologist or other therapist. The role of the psychiatrist is multiple: he or she can make a diagnosis, decide if there are other disorders present (such as depression), and will take an overall view on the disorder from a medical, psychological and social perspective.

The difference between a psychologist and psychiatrist may be summed up by saying that psychiatrists are interested in mental illness and psychologists in normal and abnormal mental processes. In reality there is a certain degree of overlap in roles. The way in which a multi-disciplinary team functions is beyond the scope of this book but the psychiatrist – as a doctor – does have some of the responsibility for overseeing the patient's progress and may have to make tough decisions, for instance with regard to the need for hospitalisation. It is difficult to wear both this hat and that of psychotherapist and thus these roles are generally divided out between team members. In situations where the team do not have the opportunity to meet formally as a team, written and telephone communication are essential at intervals in the patient's treatment.

It is not always the case that 'the more the merrier'. While medical, dietetic and psychological input are very desirable, the majority of patients do not need occupational therapy. Art therapy may be a useful alternative to talking forms of psychotherapy but should be utilised instead of rather than as well as. Too much psychotherapy with different therapists usually results in the patient avoiding real psychological work on various issues. In some centres there may be limited psychology resources and nurse therapists may deliver psychotherapy effectively.

The general practitioner plays a vital role in the process. He or she is well-placed to monitor the patient medically. The general practitioner may be able to monitor the patient's weight on a regular basis, can monitor blood tests and, most importantly, may well have known the patient and his or her family for many years.

TREATMENT – IN-PATIENT OR OUT-PATIENT?

Most patients with eating disorders can be treated as out-patients. It is not clear that all patients with eating disorders need to be treated in specialised units. A minority of patients do need in-patient treatment and if staff have some training and knowledge and if nursing requirements in particular are well-communicated by the psychiatrist, potentially many of these patients may be treated in a general psychiatric ward. In some areas there may be specific child and adolescent in-patient psychiatric beds for patients in younger age groups. The majority of young adults and their families will usually want to avoid an admission to a general adult psychiatric ward in any case as this can be a traumatic experience for a young person. It must be emphasised that in-patient treatment is needed for only a minority of patients. Some patients do well in a group-therapy based residential programme for those with eating disorders; some addiction treatment centres will also treat patients with eating disorders, although these centres are more suited to those with bulimia than to patients with anorexia who are very underweight. Specialised in-patient units may obtain excellent results although such units often preselect patients with good motivation.

The guidelines in *A Vision for Change*, the document which will guide the development of Irish mental health services in the future, suggest that patients with eating disorder should be treated within their local catchment area services where possible.

The decision as to whether the patient may be treated as an in-patient or an out-patient is made by the treating team in consultation with the patient and family, although in practice it is usually the consultant psychiatrist who is best placed to make this decision. In general, patients with bulimia nervosa do not do well with in-patient treatment. Psychiatric admission may help if the binge-purge cycle is so aggressive that the patient gets no relief whatsoever from it and admission may help break the cycle. However, many bulimic patients find that once in an unfamiliar environment they can stop bingeing but that the pattern of bingeing and vomiting becomes reinstated rapidly, either on discharge or once the hospital ward environment becomes familiar. Sometimes it is necessary to admit a bulimic patient if it is considered that there is a risk of suicide.

Patients with anorexia nervosa are usually treated as out-patients, but again, admission may be necessary under certain circumstances. These include failure to gain weight on an out-patient treatment programme (the majority of patients will be given a trial of out-patient treatment), a very rapid rate of weight loss, serious medical risks associated with weight loss, or a risk of suicide. Generally speaking, the decision to admit the patient is best made after careful consideration by the treating team, often after a period of out-patient treatment during which the team can more fully assess the patient and become familiar with other relevant issues such as family dynamics. Psychiatric admission for the treatment of anorexia nervosa is a lengthy process involving (hopefully) slow weight gain over several weeks, and is not to be entered into lightly. Patients and families need to have a realistic view of what is likely to be involved and therefore need education prior to admission.

IN-PATIENT TREATMENT OF ANOREXIA NERVOS

Patients who require in-patient treatment for anorexia are almost always very underweight. All treatment programmes need to involve both weight gain and psychological change. However, with very underweight patients, psychological change is not possible without weight gain. It is simply not realistic to expect a patient who is rigidly entrenched in her eating disorder (as patients inevitably are at very low weight) to be able to do the internal psychological 'work' that is involved in psychotherapy. The treating team will therefore need to set a target weight and establish a re-feeding regime for the patient. The target weight is usually below or at the lower limit of the normal range for the patient's age and height. This is agreed at an early stage with the patient. A dietitian will then prescribe a re-feeding regime which will allow weight gain of around 2lb (1kg) per week.

Most patients find a more rapid rate of weight gain difficult to tolerate, and a relatively slow rate at least allows the patient to adjust psychologically to her new shape. The re-feeding regime is based on as normal a diet as possible; it is usual to start at around a modest 1000 kilocalories per day or even less, well below the normal calorific requirement. In chronic starvation the stomach may shrink; dramatic and sudden re-feeding may lead to medical complications, as well as to significant anxiety for the patient. The calorific content of the diet is therefore increased gradually, slowly introducing a wider repertoire of foods.

Because of the ambivalent motivation shown by most patients, it is virtually impossible to bring about weight gain without bed-rest, supervision and a regime of rewards for weight gain. In practice this means that the patient will be confined to bed rest for a large part of the admission. As the patient gains weight, privileges such as time up out of bed, going for walks, going out with visitors may be awarded. However, when a patient is in the firm grip of anorexia, it is likely that time out of bed will be used to exercise furiously and therefore avoid weight gain. This only prolongs the patient's stay in hospital.

Some treatment units use a rigid programme of rewards for weight gain, or sanctions for failure to gain weight. Most general psychiatric units will use a less rigidly prescriptive programme, but the principles are similar. Close supervision is an essential feature of all in-patient treatment programmes. In practice this may mean that the patient requires one-to-one nursing; certainly mealtimes and the hour after meals will need supervision as patients may use all sorts of subterfuge to avoid eating, or to exercise after meals. The author has seen a variety of ingenious methods used to fool staff, including concealing food under the mattress, doing press-ups under the sheets, and of course going to the bathroom immediately after eating.

In certain rare circumstances it may be necessary to consider admitting the person against his or her will. In Ireland this means using the Mental Health Act. It must be emphasised that this occurs in very rare circumstances. In practice, patients will often concede to the wishes of their family and treating team in this situation, and may eventually agree to enter hospital under a degree of protest, reflecting the ambivalence they have towards weight gain and recovery. Specialist residential treatment programmes treat patients on a voluntary basis only because a prerequisite for such a programme is some degree of self-motivation. All detentions are subject to investigation by a Mental Health tribunal which will have the ultimate say regarding whether or not the patient's detention was legal. It may surprise some readers that people under the age of eighteen (unless they are or have been married) are considered to be minors under the Mental Health Act and can therefore be admitted to hospital with their parents' wishes without using the Mental Health Act. However, as already commented, the decision to admit a young person is a major one and would only be taken after careful consideration of its benefits vis-à-vis its risks.

The Mental Health Act contains very specific guidelines which restrict the situations in which detention can be used. The patient must be suffering from a mental disorder (this is tightly defined in the act – alcoholism for instance, does not qualify). The patient must be in reasonably imminent danger of harming herself or others if she is not admitted to hospital, or it must be the case that her judgement is so impaired that she is likely to deteriorate if not admitted to hospital. The argument that all patients with anorexia nervosa are slowly killing themselves and therefore should all be detained is against the spirit of the Mental Health Act and does not hold water. In practice, detention is reserved for very limited circumstances, such as failure to gain weight despite very extreme weight loss, a very rapid rate of weight loss or imminent medical danger (this would usually be from low potassium, low blood sugar or hypothermia) secondary to very extreme weight loss. Detaining a patient for treatment does not usually help to develop a therapeutic relationship, and can reinforce the patient's feeling of helplessness and loss of control. Patients who persist in losing weight despite best efforts as out-patients tend to invoke anxiety and a wish to 'do something' on the part of clinicians, so that the patient becomes the 'doee' and the clinician the 'doer'. Once some degree of weight gain has been established this relationship has to be redrawn, with the patient taking more responsibility for her own recovery. This is more difficult, but not impossible, if the patient has been detained against her will. It could also be argued that a patient in the grip of anorexia nervosa has the right to the opportunity to gain weight and glimpse recovery, even if at the time she expresses a wish to continue to lose weight or remain at an extremely low weight.

As one cannot force someone to eat, the main advantage conferred by having the patient detained involuntarily is that naso-gastric (tube) feeding can be used. This is an unpleasant experience for the patient and reinforces her overwhelming feeling of being unable to control her life. Generally, naso-gastric feeding, if needed, should be used for as short a time as possible. One of the aims of treatment is to assist the patient in developing a more normal relationship with food and this is clearly not possible while the patient is getting her nutrition through a tube. naso-gastric tubes can be pulled out of course, and a patient in these circumstances may require around-the-clock supervision. It must be emphasised again that these are rare circumstances; most patients who require in-patient treatment do not need to detained against their will and do not require any form of invasive treatment, although by the same token the majority are usually ambivalent about letting go their strict control of food intake.

Rapid weight gain is inadvisable and usually causes the patient to become very anxious. The slow rate of weight gain of around 2lb (1kg) per week is better tolerated and allows the patient to adapt mentally to some degree to her new shape. Some patients will try to gain weight quickly in order to get out of hospital as soon as possible – these patients are usually planning to lose that weight just as quickly. Rapid weight gain should not occur on a well-planned calorie regime developed by a dietitian. It is not a good idea for families, however well-intentioned, to bring in additional foods for the patient. This will be discouraged by hospital staff as it prevents them from supervising the prescribed diet adequately and reinforces the emotional ties that have developed around easting within the family. Families need to leave the food aspect of treatment to the staff – if the patient is failing to gain weight, this must be addressed by staff rather than families trying to make up the weight for the patient by bringing in extra food treats and so on.

The weight-increasing regime in hospital means that most patients will be in-patients for around twelve weeks. During this time, if all goes well, one would expect to see the patient being allowed increasing freedom and privileges as she gains weight. There is no point, however, in a patient being allowed to walk around a ward or hospital grounds if she is not gaining weight and in this case, the patient should be on bed rest. Most in-patient regimes involve weekly weighing-in in order to confirm that weight gain really is happening. Some patients may prepare for this by drinking gallons of water beforehand or, in one case encountered by the author, even adding lead weights to the hem of their pyjamas. However, such subterfuges do not cover up a lack of weight gain forever and staff will generally be wise to them.

The above may suggest that in-patient treatment involves a battle between treating staff and a recalcitrant patient. This is not the case – it might be better described as an attempt by staff and patient to work together against a cunning and destructive disease. One advantage of in-patient treatment is that it gives the patient an opportunity to look at her illness and its impact on her life, and perhaps at how it developed and how she might loosen its hold on her. Psychological treatment is therefore part and parcel of in-patient treatment. However, it is important for families in particular to be aware that any form of psychotherapy cannot be 'done to' or 'given to' a patient but is, rather, 'done with'. Unless the patient participates herself, psychotherapy cannot occur.

In practice, it is not possible to work psychotherapeutically with a very underweight patient, and psychological work may have to wait until the patient has gained a certain amount of weight. Likewise, psychological change does not occur overnight, or even in weeks. Psychological work that is done in an in-patient setting is only a start on something that should continue for quite some time after discharge. Therefore, patients and families must have realistic expectations of in-patient or indeed of any treatment regime. Years of abnormal eating cannot be changed in a matter of weeks. Psychotherapy at this stage may involve nothing more than gentle exploration with the patient of the meaning of the disorder, the way in which it developed, why it developed when it did, and so on. Cognitive work looking at the rigid thinking patterns that tend to be associated with anorexia may also be useful at this stage.

Many patients with anorexia nervosa find it difficult to express emotions and may be more comfortable with non-verbal forms of psychotherapy such as art therapy. It is often only much later that patients can do deep psychological work – indeed this may only really occur when the patient has moved on from the eating disorder for some years.

OUT-PATIENT TREATMENT

The majority of patient with anorexia nervosa can be treated as out-patients. Most anorexics do not wish to spend twelve weeks of their lives in hospital and this prospect alone can act as a motivator for recovery as an out-patient. The principles of treatment are the same as for in-patient treatment – steady weight gain, improved diet and psychological change. As with in-patient treatment, a team of professionals may be involved. Regular monitoring of physical health is important; this may be most appropriately done by the general practitioner. There should be agreement between the professionals involved as to who is responsible for monitoring weight gain – ideally, the patient should be weighed regularly, perhaps weekly, fortnightly or monthly – clearly this can be done by any of the professionals involved in treatment but should be done by only one, and by the same professional consistently.

All involved in treatment need to be aware of the anorexic's capacity for subterfuge and splitting. Family support is essential whether the anorexic is being treated as an out-patient or an in-patient. Families will require considerable advice and psychological support around dealing with mealtimes and conflict and avoiding enabling or taking personal responsibility away from the anorexic. The treating team, and particularly the psychiatrist, must provide leadership in this regard. For much of the duration of an anorexic's 'trajectory', it may be appropriate for the family to detach and to hand over responsibility to the anorexic. However, there may also be times when a more proscriptive approach is required – when the patient is unable to release the hold of anorexia to the extent that it is potentially life-threatening, more radical action such as insisting on hospital-isation may be necessary.

TREATMENT OF BULIMIA NERVOSA

The majority of patients with bulimia nervosa may be treated as out-patients and in-patient treatment is rare. The principles of treatment are similar as for anorexia nervosa. Again, a multi-disciplinary team is the ideal and most patients require medical monitoring, monitoring of mood and other psychopathology, dietetic guidance and psychological work. The most robust evidence for psychological work is for cognitive-behavioural therapy.

The focus in this form of therapy is on the thinking patterns and cognitive 'sets' that tend both to generate and to result from repeated bingeing and vomiting. Many patients with bulimia are engaged in a prolonged attempt to lose weight and tend to measure their self-worth in terms of whether or not they have managed to stick to a reduced calorie diet. Hence, a 'good' day for the active bulimic would be a low-calorie one, while a 'bad' day would involve eating 'forbidden foods'. As the disorder progresses, the bulimic's self-imposed rules become more rigid and therefore untenable. Straying from the reduced calorie pathway means breaking her self-imposed rules and is likely to result in a binge.

Cognitive-behavioural therapy involves both behavioural change – sticking to a healthier, normal and regular diet – and cognitive change, addressing the distorted thinking, rigid rules and faulty measures of self-worth. In reality, broader issues relating to family, childhood, relationships and so on are likely to arise in psychotherapy, even if the focus is on cognitions and behaviours. Cognitive-behavioural therapy could be described as focusing on current conscious patterns. Psychodynamic psycho-therapy focuses on the interaction between the unconscious and the conscious, the past and the present. Most psychiatrists, psychologists and psychotherapists in reality use a combination of both in the treatment of anorexia and bulimia.

In anorexia it is often extremely difficult to do deep psychotherapy until the patient has gained a certain amount of weight. In bulimia, where patients are of normal weight, there may be some potential for this type of psychological work, although this depends on the patient's motivation and ability to tolerate painful feelings which tend to arise in psychotherapy. Families, probably because of the intense anxiety and frustration provoked by eating disorders, often have a fantasy that if the therapist can only expose and probe for traumatic childhood experiences in sessions, the patient will have a catharsis or release, and be cured. This is not the case and in both anorexia and bulimia, any form of psychological treatment is a slow process with no easy cure or guaranteed results. Nonetheless, many patients do improve and over time, manage to release the hold of the eating disorder in order to get on with normal living.

3

Psychological Treatments for Eating Disorders

Gillian Moore-Groarke, Consultant Psychologist

Effective assessment, treatment and management of eating disorders typically requires a multi-disciplinary approach. The eating disorders referred to in this chapter are anorexia nervosa, bulimia nervosa and compulsive overeating. Anorexia is present when there is a significant loss of weight through food restriction and patterns of excessive exercise may also exist. Anorexics consider themselves fat even when grossly emaciated and almost skeletal. They have a phobic fear of weight gain which unfortunately sustains the condition.

Bulimic patients are usually within or above the BMI (body mass index). They regularly abuse laxatives and vomit after overeating or binge-eating in an attempt to control their weight. They fluctuate between periods of extreme starvation and compulsive bingeing and vomiting.

Compulsive eating can feel like bulimia except that sufferers do not vomit or take laxatives. Their eating is generally chaotic and out of control. They constantly are looking for the quick solution. They regularly eat in secret and experience huge guilt.

Most treatments involve a fundamental combination of appropriate psychological intervention, nutritional counselling and medical management. Medical management may or may not include consultations with a psychiatrist, depending on the aetiology and complications of the presenting symptomatology. Major treatment options for eating disorders include the following:

Hospitalisation
This is indicated in severe cases where a patient may be experiencing medical danger from severe and extreme weight loss, from excessive bingeing and purging, or where there is a risk of self-harm, severe depression or substance abuse. Unfortunately, in Ireland the number of hospital beds available for eating disorders is limited and without an appropriate hospital programme the revolving-door syndrome of discharge and readmission becomes inevitable.

Day-treatment programmes
Much of the literature on eating disorders has shown the effectiveness of day-treatment facilities. This type of programme can provide a structure around meal-time and patients are discharged home each evening. So far this option has not been utilised to its full potential in this country. This option is clearly more cost-effective than long in-patient stays.

Out-patient treatment programmes
Because of the high cost and disruption to a patient's usual life pattern associated with in-patient programmes, out-patient treatment has become popular. Here in Cork this is the facility we offer, provided we can liaise with a patient's general practitioner. Where appropriate, additional referrals to health professionals such as psychiatrists and dietitians are made.

There are several out-patient treatments that have been shown to be effective, and some of these will be discussed in more detail throughout the chapter. They include family therapy, cognitive behavioural therapy (CBT), interpersonal psychotherapy and educational approaches such as nutritional counselling and self-help treatment.

Many people who suffer from eating disorders tell themselves how much 'they feel alone'. I often hear patients say that their problem is too hard to talk about. They feel nobody understands. In time patients will recognise that other sufferers share their fears, behaviours and feelings. Many of the patients I treat feel a great sense of relief once they begin to open up about the symptoms of their eating disorder, the causes and its psychological effects. It is crucial for patients to realise that they are not alone.

Some people recover in a relatively short period of time but I have also worked with older patients who have struggled with their eating disorder for decades. The age of onset can vary from young children to adolescents to middle-aged adults, usually in reaction to upsetting life events.

Eating disorders are complex illnesses that arise from a combination of psychological and socio-cultural factors with serious consequences for mental and physical health. Sadly, eating disorders have the potential to be life threatening.

COGNITIVE BEHAVIOURAL THERAPY (CBT)
CBT is the treatment of choice for many sufferers of eating disorders whose symptoms are moderate to severe. The therapy is aimed at correcting errors in thinking and perception that lead to negative perceptions of one's self and subsequent symptomatology of an eating disorder.

CBT is a way of talking about:

- How you think about yourself, the world and those around you.
- How what you do affects your thoughts and feelings.

CBT can help you to change how you think (the cognitive) and what you do (the behaviour). These changes can make you feel much better. CBT focuses on the 'here and now' of presenting problems and difficulties. Rather than dwelling on the distress caused by the various symptomatology of the disorder in the past, it encourages the patient to look at ways of improving their state of mind *now*.

CBT is aimed at normalising eating behaviour and reducing restrictive eating by slowly re-introducing the so called 'taboo' foods into the new healthy eating plan. The therapy involves the patient playing a proactive role in his/her recovery, with daily self-monitoring of food intake, bingeing and purging episodes and the thoughts and feelings that trigger destructive eating patterns. CBT also involves regular weighing and discussion with the psychologist around changes in weight.

A brief history of CBT

Many people think that cognitive therapy is a relatively recent development. In fact, behaviour therapy was developed in the 1950s and 1960s, when clinical psychologists learned about experiments on animal and humans that showed how behaviour can be changed and controlled. They decided to apply their laboratory findings to patients with behavioural problems.

Cognitive therapy was developed by US psychiatrist Aaron

T. Beck in the early 1960s. Beck's approach initially focused on research into the treatment of depression but in the last two decades cognitive therapy has been applied to an increasing number of disorders. Cognitive therapy is the most popular and best validated approach for eating disorders.

Cognitive therapists presume that the maladaptive cognitions associated with eating disorders may arise from faulty social learning; from a lack of experiences that would allow adaptive learning (i.e. development of appropriate coping skills and strategies); from dysfunctional family experiences; or from traumatic events or experiences.

How does CBT work?
CBT can help you to make sense of overwhelming problems by breaking them down into smaller parts to make it easier to see how they are connected and how they affect you.

- Thoughts (patterns of thinking)
- Emotions (how we feel)
- Physical reactions/symptoms
- Action (what we do)

Each of these areas can affect the others in varying ways. How you think about a problem can affect how you feel physically and emotionally. It can also alter your action or actions (what you do about it).

There are helpful and unhelpful ways of reacting to most situations depending on how you think about them.

SITUATION You have had a bad day bingeing. Your partner is aware of this and ignores you all evening.	
Thoughts (unhelpful) He doesn't like me anymore.	*Thoughts (helpful)* Maybe he has had a bad day too. There might be something upsetting him.
Emotional feelings (unhelpful) Sad, disgusted rejected	*Emotional feelings (helpful)* Concerned for other person
Physical (unhelpful) Low energy, nauseated, stomach cramps	*Physical (helpful)* None – feel OK
Negative Action Continue to avoid unhelpful feelings.	*Positive Action* Request time to talk and communicate what is going on for you and listen to your partner.

You can see from this example that the same situation can lead to two very different ways of thinking. How you think affects how you feel and the action(s) you subsequently take.

Unhelpful thinking makes you jump to a conclusion based on no evidence. You may:

- Have several uncomfortable feelings
- Engage in many destructive and unhelpful behaviours

CBT is a very active type of therapy. It teaches you a number of things about your illness, its symptoms and how to predict when symptoms will most likely recur.

Through the use of the daily thought record (see Appendix 1) you keep a diary of eating episodes, binge-eating, purging and the events that may have triggered these episodes.

With the help of the dietitian in nutritional counselling, you draw up an eating plan that helps you to eat more regularly, with meals and snacks spaced appropriately.

You also learn that you control the symptoms of your illness, based on the choices you make. Once you change your incorrect beliefs about your symptoms this reduces the 'perceived power' the symptoms have over you.

Automatic thought patterns that are self-defeating and negative automatic thought patterns disappear. Changing your destructive thoughts improves your mood, gives you a new sense of mastery over your life and reduces or ends the development of future episodes of destructive symptomatology. Methods of handling the events and problems of daily life become more effective. Appropriate handling of problems is apt to reduce the likelihood of a recurrence of the illness.

CBT helps to change non-effective behaviours into effective actions for dealing with symptoms. Changing behaviours often changes the frequency and severity of prolonged episodes of the illness. CBT also helps to reduce a patient's concerns and fears about physical symptoms that develop during emotional stress (panic attacks for example). Prophylactic use of relaxation therapy combined with CBT is extremely beneficial. It can help the anorexic to overcome the phobic state of fear around food, reduce bingeing/purging among bulimics and reduce episodes of overeating among obese patients or comfort eaters.

The five areas diagram

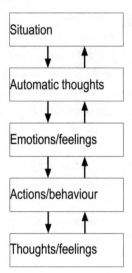

This diagram is a simple way of looking at what happens. The whole sequence or parts of it can have enormous influence. It can become a never-ending vicious circle where the 'food becomes the enemy' and acts as the symptom and not the cause of the eating disorder.

Destructive relationships around food represent a transference of control. Through CBT the therapist teaches you to break the vicious circle of altered thinking, feelings and behaviours. Once you begin to see parts of the sequence clearly you can begin the process of changing the way you feel.

You eventually learn to become your own therapist. You can 'do it yourself': work out your own way of tackling the problems that come your way. If you improve one area of your life you are likely to have the courage to improve other areas of your life.

There are four main CBT techniques that I use with patients:

1.   FOOD DIARIES

With eating disorder patients, food diaries are often the first step to behaviour change. At the end of each assessment meeting I always ask patients to record how much they eat and what happened before and after their eating. In CBT this is called the ABC approach:

> A: events/emotions before eating
> B: behaviour: the amount of food you ate and how you ate
> C: consequences: what you felt, thought or did after eating

On the next page is an example of a food diary by a bulimic patient. The purpose of the diary is to find out what happens before and after eating. I always find this useful to help design programmes with patients to help them change their eating behaviour. Generally, feedback from patients indicates that it makes them more aware of the situations and behavioural consequences that are related to their eating problems. The diary helps you to learn which situations you eat in and don't eat in. You also discover which situations are least comfortable for you. If filled out honestly a food diary can provide an accurate, detailed description of how much you actually eat.

Date	A	B	C
01.06.07	Went to friend's birthday party.	Ate 3/4 bites. Played with my food.	1. Felt bad my friend paid. 2. Relieved nobody said anything.
02.06.07	Alone in the house.	Binged on three bowls of cereal	1. Disappointed that I broke out. 2. Walked 2 miles
03.06.07	Felt as if I was going to faint.	Ate six bags of Tayto.	1. Felt it could have been worse. 2. Took laxatives.

2   REWARD SYSTEMS

Once a patient begins to engage in therapy I usually compile with them a list of rewards. We can then go about setting food goals. If the patient fulfils a goal he/she earns the reward. For example, Tim's Mum agreed to pay money towards his school trip to New York each day that he drank a can of a nutritional shake. If he succeeded for a week an additional amount was added to his 'fund'. As treatment progressed his food goals changed and more foods were gradually added to Tim's food plan. He was also encouraged to engage in 'spontaneous' or unplanned eating with friends for example at the cinema or watching a DVD. Initially, he found this very difficult but over time he began to trust himself.

The CBT reward system is a good short-term solution but emphasis must also be placed on valued living and healthy eating rather than short-term reward goals.

3.   EXPOSURE

Exposure is a common technique used in CBT. I usually ask patients to make a list of uncomfortable situations directly related to eating (e.g. eating dinner at a friend's house, going to a restaurant, being unsure what is on a menu, using a scales to be weighed, looking in a mirror, looking at a photograph of oneself…)

Usually, we begin with the least-feared behaviour, using relaxation therapy to soften the effects of the exposure. The ultimate goal of exposure is to reduce your level of discomfort.

4   THOUGHT-CHANGING

The goal of thought-changing is to help you to change or eliminate some of the thoughts you experience. Struggling with an eating disorder can lend itself to excessive thinking about food, body shape and weight. Such thought processes consume enormous amounts of mental energy. Eating disorder patients frequently engage in the following patterns of thinking:

All or nothing thinking

Thinking you have it all or nothing: 'If I don't have a size 10 body I'm totally gross' or 'Unless I can wear size 10, I will not go out in public.'

Personalisation

Taking things too personally: 'I know people in the restaurant are looking and laughing at me.'

Magnification

Believing that eating or weight gain will have catastrophic consequences: 'If I gain 2lbs no one will ever like me' or 'I feel my stomach and body will explode when I eat.'

Superstitious thinking
Connecting food to events in an unrealistic way: 'I will not get the job because the candidate before me was skinny.'

As part of the thought-changing technique you ask yourself what evidence you have to support your negative thought patterns. This allows you to check the accuracy of your thoughts and eventually with the help of a therapist, the patient will recognise the logical flaws in their thoughts and replace inaccurate thoughts with more appropriate ones.

Using continuum scales is also useful. For example, Gemma said to me one day, 'If I'm not in complete control of my food, I feel my life is totally out of control.' You can challenge these maladaptive thoughts by asking yourself to measure approximately the amount to which you genuinely subscribe to the thought on a continuum of 0 per cent to 100 per cent.

Gemma eventually learned that despite difficulties with her eating, she was still in control of her job and her role as a mother and wife. The goal of thought-changing is to increase the good thoughts and decrease the bad/negative thought processes.

HOW EFFECTIVE IS COGNITIVE BEHAVIOURAL THERAPY?
CBT can be done individually or with a group of people. Usually patients are well on their way to recovery before I encourage them to engage in group therapy.

Usually, if you attend individually, you meet your therapist on a regular basis, weekly or fortnightly to begin with. Each session lasts between thirty and forty-five minutes. The first two to four sessions will involve the therapist checking with you that you are comfortable with this type of treatment and that you are willing to engage in the homework exercises.

You will also be asked questions about your past life and background. Although CBT concentrates on the 'here and now', at times you may need to enter the past to discover how it has affected the present. I often say to patients that it is necessary 'to go back to move forward'. The patient agrees the agenda, and identifies the issues they want to address in the short, medium and long term. This is usually contracted in the first few sessions. An initial assessment form provides useful information for the therapist and patient (see Appendix 2).

The work involves breaking each problem down into its separate parts. You and the therapist will look at the five areas discussed in the diagram on page 80. You will examine how helpful or unhelpful your thoughts are and how they affect each other and you.

The therapist helps you to work out how to change unhelpful thoughts and behaviours. At each meeting you will review your progress from the last session. You can renegotiate some of the tasks if they seem too hard or don't seem to be helping you. You decide the pace of treatment and what you will and won't try. The main advantage of CBT is that you can continue to put into practice what you have learned long after sessions have finished. Many patients have confided in me that they have applied CBT techniques to several other areas of their lives once they have mastered the basic techniques.

If a patient is not willing to carry out the homework exercises, CBT will not work for them, so another type of talking therapy may work more effectively. Much research has shown that CBT combined with medication can be effective for quite severe cases. Vigilant practitioners will avoid the use of medication, particularly in young adolescent patients, and encourage the use of medical monitoring by a GP combined with regular CBT and nutrition counselling.

CBT is considered very effective for the long-term treatment of eating disorders. Because eating disorders can endure for a long period of time, ongoing psychological treatment is usually required for a number of years.

In a recent survey in my practice the average duration of treatment from start to finish was found to be eighteen months. For CBT to be effective you need to work in cooperation with your therapist towards agreed goals.

FAMILY THERAPY

Family therapy is a highly effective treatment for eating disorders. It works effectively alongside individual therapy and medical and nutritional monitoring. The success of family-based treatment has been highlighted significantly in literature on eating disorders.

One patient described family therapy:

> …as often hard to go through, hating to tell your innermost feelings to your loved ones. At one session I wrote a letter to each of them, and the aftermath was not easy, letting my father know that I wanted to choose my own career path and not his. It was such a learning experience.

In a study conducted by Russell et al in 1987, family therapy was shown to be highly effective and necessary in most cases, especially in cases where the patient was still living at home. Eating disorders create high emotional stress that is usually echoed by all family members. Among siblings and parents such 'expression of emotions' through eating disorders can create strong negative and critical attitudes. Unfortunately this can have an adverse effect on the progress of the patient.

Families need to be taught to come together with the patient to identify the stressors and learn effective communication and problem-solving skills. In severe cases where there are dysfunctional interactions occurring among family members, temporary constructive separations may be implemented. Family support groups are also effective in helping families to overcome feelings of isolation, discuss problems and set realistic goals about their individual cases.

The goal of family therapy is to focus on assisting the family to work together in overcoming the eating disorder. Incorporating family or in some cases marital therapy into a patient's care may help prevent relapses by resolving interpersonal issues related to the eating disorder. The therapist can guide family members in understanding the patient's disorder and learning new techniques for coping with problems.

Depending on the severity of family dysfunction, treatment for some patients may need to be long-term. Family therapy will be dependent on an individual's family situation so its application will differ from case to case.

Parents tend to be the first people to diagnose the eating disorders, primarily because they show up around kitchen tables and in family bathrooms. Everybody who comes into contact with the individual suffers: parents, siblings, grandparents – and in some cases friends and teachers.

Recovery also happens over time within the family home. The patient has to learn to apply what they learn in therapy within the family dynamics. Patients typically spend 30-45 minutes a week in therapy or with their doctor. The rest of the time is spent at work, at home or at school. Naturally the nature of parental involvement will vary according to the age and needs of the patient. The readiness of parents, partners and siblings to be open contributes significantly to recovery. Essentially a major goal is learning to reconnect within an agreed framework of appropriate rules and boundaries.

Often the patient requires autonomy from parents but ultimately the benefits of combined family and individual therapy greatly outweigh the short-term difficulties in acknowledging the need for change.

Feelings of anger, distress, guilt, fear, anxiety and mistrust are some of the many emotions that come up in family sessions. Mothers who themselves have struggled with issues of food suffer great guilt.

Here is a mother's first hand account of her sixteen-year-old son's fight with anorexia nervosa:

'When the first doctor identified Ted's problem, we were convinced that he was over-reacting. Ted had developed a huge interest in food and exercise before and after giving up rowing. When the second doctor recommended that we see a psychologist, as a preventative measure, we went along with it.

'The first meeting was a shock. After speaking to Ted, the psychologist told us Ted had a serious problem. I remember blaming myself and my interest in food, cooking and nutrition. I wondered how he would have been if I had not been his mother. I bought every book I could find on the subject of anorexia and devoured every detail.

'One key issue for Ted was growth. He suddenly understood that his malnourished body would not achieve its full height potential if he did not eat enough.

'However much he tried. Ted could not eat enough. Every bite required careful consideration and discussion, in person or by text. I remember one awful Friday, in January, driving 400 miles in the rain, for a meeting, stopping on the way to answer texts from Ted about how much to eat, all the time being scared that the school would phone to ask us to take him home. He was unable to concentrate properly, he was obsessed with himself, he was always cold and he was unable to exert himself.

'I remember panicking one night, looking at his emaciated body, thinking that he was going to have to go to hospital and once there, he would not be coming back.

It was when he was asked to sit out a PE class that the PE teacher chatted to him and then phoned us. Ted had told him his diagnosis. The teacher wanted to let us know that he was there to help and was willing to talk with Ted whenever he needed to talk. We suggested that he inform the principal, if he thought it wise, but suggested keeping the information only for those teachers who needed to know.

'It was critical that we saw the psychologist as soon as we did. This came about by asking for a cancellation appointment. Similarly, when the psychologist recommended a dietitian, we got a cancelled appointment.

'The dietitian proved the turning point. We had kept a food diary for the psychologist the previous week and from that she devised a meal plan for Ted. On the way home he insisted that we immediately buy as many of the items as possible to enable him to start the plan straight away. Once he started, Ted stuck rigidly to the meal plan. He ate excruciatingly slowly but he ate it all. It seemed like mountains of food, compared with what he had been eating.

'The following evening, we brought him for a massage.

After months of tension, his body relaxed and he learnt to sleep properly.

'Ted no longer thought about food as there were no food decisions to make. Over the next few weeks he met the psychologist weekly. He steadily gained weight. The psychologist seemed to be sorting through issues with him. I met her briefly at the end of each session. He was confiding in her and no longer talking to us at all. This was a difficult stage for us, having been so close to him, to be suddenly excluded from his concerns and feelings.

'Family therapy was a significant part of the treatment programme. A difficult family therapy session drew out some profound issues, but cleared the air and set us on a new road to better family relations. Months later the benefit is clear: a more balanced family relationship between parents and children.

'Although Ted is considered well recovered from anorexia nervosa, he still has to deal with teenage issues. He eats well and is growing steadily. He is content, as much as a teenager can be. We know that we were very fortunate to have caught the illness early and to have found the best professional care for him. We even consider that having been through this experience, he has actually benefited in the long run. He has faced issues which might never have been dealt with, or which might have arisen later in his life and been more difficult to deal with then. The psychologist's recent advice has been like coaching, setting him career guidance and helping him to focus realistically on his future and the steps required to achieve his goals. Ted is looking forward now and so are we.'

Family roles

Roles play an extremely important part in an emotionally healthy family dynamic. Family roles are patterns of behaviour by which family members individually and together fulfil family functions and needs.

In examining the roles of the family the therapist may be met with some resistance at first. Parents often feel the process can be somewhat intrusive, so great sensitivity is necessary.

Researchers refer to five main family roles as being essential:

- Provider of basic needs: resources such as food, money, clothing and shelter.
- Nurturer and emotional support-provider: supporting family members in an effective manner to provide psychological comfort and reassurance.
- Life coach: teaching of social skills, social intervention, career choices and decision-making
- Family manager: this involves leadership, financial management, discipline and enforcing behavioural standards.
- Intimacy provider: among the adults a satisfying sexual relationships is one of the keys to a quality partnership.

The family can help to develop healthy roles using the following methodology.

- Establish clear roles with appropriate boundaries for and between parents and children.
- Allow flexibility of roles that will change in response to changed circumstances.

- Allocate roles fairly.
- Be responsible in your role and consider others.
- Focus on the family's strengths rather than its weaknesses.

PSYCHOLOGICAL DISORDERS THAT COEXIST WITH EATING DISORDERS

Depression is the most common disorder that can occur with eating disorders

Obsessive compulsive disorder (OCD)

This is an anxiety disorder in which individuals feel compelled to engage in endless rituals to reduce disturbing and frightening thoughts they feel they cannot control. The eating disorder patient may set rules for food preparation and eat only foods cut in a particular shape to rid themselves of unwanted thoughts that are focused on weight. One of my patients once said to me: 'My obsessive compulsive disorder is quite peculiar, I have to organise every single thing ritualistically and when something is even slightly out of balance, I can only feel sadness and aggression'.

Post traumatic stress disorder (PTSD)

This is a response to being in a traumatic life-or-death situation. Among female patients sexual assault can lead to PTSD and subsequent eating disorders. Other triggers which relate to PTSD are road traffic accidents, witnessing crimes or natural disasters. Weight control is often a way of disguising flashbacks and painful thoughts and feelings about the trauma. The sense of helplessness and victimisation is replaced by 'food the enemy'.

Drug and alcohol abuse

Substance abuse is found to be common particularly among bulimic and overweight patients. These patients are usually less compliant with treatment programmes. Generally, we recommend that the substance abuse is treated first unless a patient's health is in grave danger from the eating disorder. Cross-addiction is quite common among those who suffer from eating disorders.

THE QUESTION WHY?

Every day in clinical practice we are asked why do people go to such great extremes to control their weight. Why do people continue with the war against 'food the enemy'. While the media have a certain influence on how we look, ultimately *we* make the choice to continue fighting the battle with food. Why do so many people devote all their attention and energy to food? The most common influences are categorised as follows:

Sociocultural influences

Society bombards us with the message that we should be thin. We are encouraged to believe that if we want to be accepted and liked we must be thin. In general, Western culture applauds thinness.

A feeling of lack of control

We cannot control all the things that happen to us in our lives. People with eating disorders, especially anorexia nervosa and bulimia nervosa, feel that restrictive eating allows them to regain control of their life. An obese patient I recently treated felt she too had regained control of her life, having spent nine weeks on Lipotrim© shakes. This lady required immediate referral to a dietitian. 'Hot thoughts' which represent cognitive distortions such as: 'Eating less gives me a sense of being in total control' or 'I'm so proud of not eating food for two weeks; I have my control back' are all too common. It is always a good exercise to get a patient to make a list of things he or she would like to control but cannot control. The feelings associated with these examples can form the basis of good therapy sessions and help a patient to focus on more realistic goals.

Family dynamics
Early research blamed families and especially mothers who were overprotective for the onset of eating disorders. There is still some evidence that family problems do contribute to many eating-disordered behaviours. Parenting is a very challenging role for many of us to undertake, as children do not come with clear instructions!

Hereditary factors
Eating disorders are often hereditary and if one member of your family has had an issue around weight there is a chance that another member of the family can also develop an eating disorder. Weight is based on age, height, sex and build, and many factors need to be taken into account.

Perfectionism
Striving for perfectionism is never-ending because it is unattainable. Hamachek (1978) defined perfectionism as follows:

> Perfectionism usually reflects a deep seated sense of inferiority and is a learned way of reaching for approval and acceptance by setting standards for

achievement or performance that are unrealistically high. As a consequence, no effort is ever quite good enough, and that is what keeps the perfectionist neurotic…always reaching but never attaining. It is an endless cycle of self-perpetuating and defeating behaviour of trying, frustration and failure because there is no conclusion to the trying, because there is no such thing as perfection'.

CONCLUSION

While a number of triggers can be identified, nobody will ever know for sure why a patient develops an eating disorder.

The good news is you do not really have to know what caused your eating disorder to allow you to move on from it. No amount of insight into the past can take away the aetiology of the disorder. You are better to live in the here-and-now and start rebuilding your life.

Eating disorders are currently a public health challenge and while much public attention focuses on obesity, the development of specialised clinics and treatment programmes must take all eating disorders into account.

APPENDIX 1: DAILY THOUGHTS RECORD

Situation		
Automatic Thoughts	Describe clearly and concisely the thoughts that went through your mind in that situation? Rate believability of thoughts 0%–100%	
Emotions	What were you feeling? Rate intensity of emotion 0%–100%	
Alternative Responses	What might be more helpful and balanced responses to your automatic thoughts? Rate believability of responses 0%–100%	
Outcome	How do you feel now? Re-rate intensity of emotion 0%–100%	

APPENDIX 2: INITIAL ASSESSMENT SHEET

Name:

Date:

Initial Assessment

What do you see as the main problem?

Where does it occur?

When does it occur?

With whom does it occur?

What makes the problem worse?

What makes the problem better?

Analysis of a specific incident/situation related to the main problem

Describe incident/situation

Thoughts – what were you thinking?

Emotions – what were you feeling?

Behaviour – what did you do?

Physical – what symptoms did you experience?

Wider perspective of problem

Onset – when did it begin?

Course – how has the problem developed since its onset?

Predisposing factors – anything in your background that made it

likely that you would develop this problem?

Goals – clear, specific, measurable and within the client's control

to achieve

Client's expectations of therapy

4

Eating Disorders: A Dietitian's Perspective

Ann Marie Brennan, Senior Paediatric Dietitian

INTRODUCTION

In this chapter, I discuss the common nutritional issues and concerns that face young people with eating disorders and also the nutritional management of obesity among young people. It is important to bear in mind that all young people are different and recommendations need to be tailored to the situation. If there are concerns, expert advice is necessary.

Parents play a crucial role in helping their children to develop lifelong healthy eating habits. For many parents, this can be a real challenge. Parents commonly ask: what is normal eating and is my child eating enough? There are many variations in 'normal eating' that may cause concern to parents. Changes in childhood eating patterns are usually temporary. If children are growing as expected and appear to be healthy and happy, parents should readily accept these variations, as they generally do not pose a threat to health. Your GP will have charts for the normal growth and development of children and is the best person to consult if you are concerned.

Children can develop food fads, a very common phase that

occurs in the toddler years and that may last from a few months to a couple of years. The child usually grows out of this and moves on to more varied eating. Another problem may arise when a child eats a very limited range of foods, yet manages to gain weight and appears to be thriving. Parents should try not to get too anxious about this and not attempt to influence the child too strongly. It usually resolves itself over time.

What happens in the home has a major bearing on a young person's eating behaviour, food intake, body size, physical activity levels and attitudes to healthy eating. Modern society places many demands on our time. Often both parents are working and children may have after-school activities such as sports and dance classes. It can be a challenge to establish regular family meals and to avoid relying on convenience foods and snacks. Parents' own attitudes to food and health also strongly influence their child's eating habits. Children may develop an unhealthy attitude to food if lots of emphasis has been placed by parents on restricting fat or dieting for health reasons. Parental over-concern with children being thin or encouragement to avoid being fat can influence young people to become constant dieters and use unhealthy weight-control methods (Field et al, 2001).

A recent Irish survey showed that 12 per cent of Irish children were on a weight-reducing diet and another 20 per cent felt they needed to lose weight (HBSC, 2006). This clearly illustrates the level of dissatisfaction amongst Irish children with their body weight. A previous Irish survey alarmingly found 22 per cent of Irish children to be either overweight or obese (IUNA, 2005). If unhealthy eating behaviours are maintained during childhood and adolescence, they can have short- and long- term health consequences, including obesity, heart disease, osteoporosis and delayed sexual maturation.

NUTRITION

Optimal nutrition is essential for achieving your child's full growth potential. A balanced diet is required to provide the energy and nutrients necessary for good health. The main nutrients are proteins, fats, carbohydrates, vitamins and minerals.

Proteins

Proteins are found mainly in meat, poultry, fish, eggs, dairy products and nuts. They are made up of amino acids and are the body's building blocks. Children need protein for growth. Many parts of the body are made from protein: hair, skin, blood, muscles.

Fats

The body needs dietary fat and essential fatty acids (omega 3 and 6) for normal growth and development. Fats are a rich source of energy and supply the body with fat-soluble vitamins, such as vitamins A, D, E and K.

Carbohydrates

Carbohydrates are the body's main energy source. Carbohydrate-rich foods include fruit, vegetables, breads, cereals and legumes (peas, beans and lentils) and some are a good source of dietary fibre, which helps prevent constipation. Soft drinks are a major source of added sugar in the diet and are not necessary.

Vitamins and Mineral

Vitamins and minerals cannot be made by the body and therefore need to be ingested. The dietary sources of some of the main vitamins and minerals and their functions are listed on the next page.

TABLE 1: VITAMINS AND MINERALS

Nutrient	Function	Dietary Sources
Calcium	Needed for healthy bones and teeth	Dairy products: milk, yoghurts, cheese Dark green leafy vegetables Calcium-enriched foods e.g. orange juice, breakfast cereals
Vitamin D	Helps the body absorb calcium for healthy bones and teeth	Sunshine Oily fish, e.g. salmon, sardines Eggs Margarines Some fortified breakfast cereals
Vitamin C	Benefits the immune system and wound healing. Keeps skin healthy. Help the body absorb iron. Acts as an anti-oxidant.	Citrus fruits Berries and currants Vegetables such as green peppers, broccoli, cabbage.
Folate	Prevents anaemia. Prevents neural tube defects.	Green leafy vegetables Fortified foods e.g. some breakfast cereals, breads Citrus fruits and juices

Iron	Iron transports oxygen around the body. Prevents iron-deficiency anaemia	There are two forms of dietary iron: haem and non-haem. Haem sources of iron are well absorbed by the body and include meat, poultry and fish. Non-haem sources are not as well absorbed and are found in green leafy vegetables, fortified breakfast cereals. Vitamin C-rich foods improve the absorption of non-haem iron
Vitamin A	Helps keep skin healthy. Benefits the immune system. Prevents night blindness.	Liver Red and orange fruit and vegetables Oily fish Dairy products

FOOD GROUPS

A well-balanced diet can be achieved with reference to the food pyramid to help provide children with adequate energy, vitamins and minerals for optimal growth and development. Healthy eating means eating a variety of foods in the right amounts from the main food groups, as outlined in the food pyramid on the facing page (courtesy of the Department of Health and Children).

Use the Food Pyramid to plan your healthy food choices every day and watch your portion size

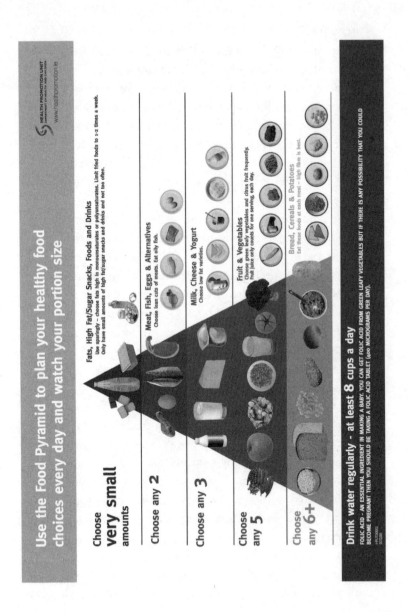

Choose very small amounts

Fats, High Fat/Sugar Snacks, Foods and Drinks
Use sparingly – choose fats high in monounsaturates or polyunsaturates. Limit fried foods to 1-2 times a week.
Only have small amounts of high fat/sugar snacks and drinks and not too often.

Choose any 2

Meat, Fish, Eggs & Alternatives
Choose lean cuts of meats. Eat oily fish.

Choose any 3

Milk, Cheese & Yogurt
Choose low fat varieties.

Choose any 5

Fruit & Vegetables
Choose green leafy vegetables and citrus fruit frequently.
Fruit juice only counts for one serving, each day.

Choose any 6+

Bread, Cereals & Potatoes
Eat these foods at each meal – high fibre is best.

Drink water regularly - at least 8 cups a day

FOLIC ACID – AN ESSENTIAL INGREDIENT IN MAKING A BABY. YOU CAN GET FOLIC ACID FROM GREEN LEAFY VEGETABLES BUT IF THERE IS ANY POSSIBILITY THAT YOU COULD BECOME PREGNANT THEN YOU SHOULD BE TAKING A FOLIC ACID TABLET (400 MICROGRAMS PER DAY).

GROWTH

A diet consisting of nutrient-rich foods such as meat, fish, eggs, fruit, vegetables, whole grain cereals and dairy products will ensure sufficient intakes of nutrients for optimal growth and bone health. The major growth spurt seen in childhood is at the beginning of adolescence and is marked by the onset of puberty. Prior to puberty, growth rates of boys and girls are quite similar and their nutrient needs are similar. Girls enter puberty before boys; boys generally start their growth spurt two years after girls.

The requirements for nutrients are at their highest during this phase of rapid growth, particularly in boys, as they grow taller and gain a greater amount of lean body mass compared to girls. The greatest gain in adolescent height occurs in the year preceding menarche (beginning of periods) for girls and at around fourteen years for boys. Girls reach their near-adult height by the age of fourteen.

Adolescents double their weight during this short period of six to eight years. The greatest gains in weight occur at thirteen years for girls and fourteen for boys.

Bones grow in length up until the late teen years and grow in strength until peak bone mass is achieved at around thirty-five years of age. The greater the peak bone mass achieved the stronger the bones, thereby reducing the risk of fractures and osteoporosis. Approximately half an individual's peak bone mass is accumulated during adolescence. By the age of eighteen as much as 90 per cent of adult bone calcium will be laid down in the skeleton.

Adolescents experience significant physical changes in their bodies during puberty. It can be difficult for teenagers, particularly adolescent girls, to cope with the dramatic changes in body shape and size. While gaining body fat mass is a normal and essential process, is often viewed negatively by adolescent girls. Poor body image and dissatisfaction with body weight often lead to dieting, which can lead to unhealthy weight-control behaviours, for example use of diet pills or laxatives, disordered eating and ultimately eating disorders such as anorexia nervosa and bulimia nervosa.

WHEN SHOULD EATING BEHAVIOURS BECOME A CAUSE FOR CONCERN?

Eating disorders such as anorexia nervosa and bulimia nervosa are psychological problems and are more associated with distorted body image and a negative view of oneself rather than with food and eating. These feelings and emotions associated with food are very variable and are sometimes associated with control and deprivation. In certain children, food and eating assume an abnormal significance and rather than eat in response to hunger or appetite, they use eating or not eating to help block out painful or uncomfortable thoughts and feelings.

Eating disorders commonly develop during adolescence so it is important to observe your child's attitudes/behaviours to food and weight. You might notice some of the following attitudes or behaviours:

- Feels fat
- Poor self-image
- Frequent weight checks
- Weight loss
- Uses the bathroom frequently during or after meals
- Denies hunger
- Avoids family mealtimes

- Interested in preparing meals but avoids eating them
- Displays restrictive eating habits, eating limited variety of foods
- Avoids eating out in restaurants
- Lots of anxiety and upset expressed around mealtimes

EATING DISORDERS

There are many factors that play an important role in the development of eating disorders. There is enormous societal pressure to strive to be thin, as thinness is strongly associated with attractiveness. Children are growing up in a culture that promotes restrictive eating behaviours and dissatisfaction with body size and shape. They are repeatedly exposed to advertisements that encourage slimming and dieting and they have access to internet web sites that encourage eating disorders. Certain individuals may be more sensitive to environmental pressures for thinness and may feel a need to conform to a certain body size and shape.

The most widely recognised eating disorders are anorexia nervosa and bulimia nervosa. They are predominantly disorders of teenage girls and young women. However, eating disorders can occur in boys and are becoming more common in adolescent males. The sufferer of either disorder has an extreme preoccupation with weight and/or shape and an extreme fear of weight gain.

Symptoms

- Distorted body image
- Out-of-control eating
- Purging behaviours

- Intense fear of weight gain
- Denial of hunger and cravings
- Fat phobia
- Menstrual irregularity
- Loss of weight
- Restrictive eating patterns

Other symptoms:

- Wearing baggy clothes to cover up weight loss
- Extremely limited food choices
- Avoiding eating with family
- Ritualised eating habits
- Change in food rules, e.g. becoming vegetarian
- Excessive fluid (particularly water) intake

ANOREXIA NERVOSA

Girls with anorexia nervosa tend to be preoccupied with their stomachs and thighs being fat whereas boys with anorexia nervosa may be more concerned about their chest size and musculature. Within anorexia nervosa there are two subtypes: restricting and bingeing/purging. The 'restrictive subtype' of anorexia nervosa achieves weight loss through dietary restriction often coupled with excessive exercise. Alternatively purging behaviours such as self-induced vomiting or laxative abuse can be used to achieve weight loss hence known as the 'binge-purge subtype'.

Children and adolescents with anorexia nervosa may display one or many of the following characteristics:

- Intense fear of fatness
- Obsessive thinking about food

- Intense fear of weight gain
- Distorted body image
- Low mood
- Preoccupation with body size/shape
- Genuine belief that they are fat despite being underweight
- For prepubertal children, failure to gain expected weight during growth spurts is significant

BULIMIA NERVOSA

In bulimia nervosa, the sufferer lacks a sense of control over eating and experiences overwhelming urges to overeat or binge. Binge-eating is often followed by huge guilt because of the fear of gaining weight. The sufferer will often use inappropriate 'compensatory behaviours' following the binge episodes to compensate for the extra calorie load; purging e.g. vomiting, abuse of laxatives (binge-purge subtype), fasting and/or excessive exercise (restrictive subtype). Sufferers of bulimia nervosa may display the following characteristics:

- Extreme importance is placed on body image and weight
- Normal to overweight but some sufferers may be slightly underweight
- Restrictive eating patterns are adopted in an attempt to control weight
- Binge-eating, large quantities of food are consumed
- Purging behaviour (e.g. self-induced vomiting or laxative abuse) develops as a means of controlling the guilt felt after large binge-eating episodes

MEDICAL AND NUTRITIONAL CONSEQUENCES OF EATING DISORDERS

Medical

Eating disorders are psychiatric conditions which can lead to significant medical and nutritional complications. The adverse effects of eating disorders are numerous. They are primarily related to the effects of malnutrition and the weight-control behaviours like vomiting. In acute and severe malnutrition, there is potential to affect every organ system. Most of the medical complications caused by eating disorders in adolescents improve with nutritional rehabilitation and recovery from the eating disorder but depending on the child's stage of development some may be potentially irreversible and include:

- Growth retardation
- Pubertal delay
- Damage to brain tissue and digestive system
- Loss of dental enamel associated with vomiting
- Failure to achieve peak bone mass, predisposing to osteoporosis and increased risk of fractures

Nutritional

Nutritional deficiencies are seen in young people with eating disorders. The consequences of inadequate dietary intake are related to the duration, severity, the number of episodes of restriction and very importantly for adolescents the timing of those episodes. Inadequate energy intake makes it difficult for the body to function normally and there are many physical signs of nutritional deficiency as outlined below.

TABLE 2: PHYSICAL SIGNS ASSOCIATED WITH NUTRITIONAL DEFICIENCIES

Assessment	Physical Sign	Possible Nutrient(s) Deficiency
Bones	Osteoporosis (brittle bone disease)	Calcium, Vitamin D
Eyes	Pale conjunctiva	Iron
Gums	Spongy, bleed easily	Vitamin C
Hair	Thin, dull, dry, brittle, becomes easily pluckable	Protein-Energy
Lips	Inflammation and chapping of the lips	B Vitamins
Muscles	Wasting, weakness, fatigue	Protein-Energy
Nails	Brittle, easily broken	Iron
Skin	Dry, flaky Pale	Essential fatty acids, Iron
Subcutaneous Tissue	Loss of fat stores	Energy

Hospitalisation

Hospitalisation of children with eating disorders is necessary if there is severe malnutrition, dehydration, electrolyte disturbances or failure of out-patient treatment. In extreme cases feeding against the will of the child may be necessary in order to sustain life. In a severely malnourished patient there may be a risk of 're-feeding syndrome' which has associated medical risks: the re-feeding phase requires a gradual advancement of nutrients intake and close monitoring. However the goals of the child achieving physical and psychological wellbeing remain the same whether in a hospital ward or out-patient setting.

Nutritional Management of Eating Disorders
The care of patients with eating disorders ideally involves the expertise and dedication of a multi-disciplinary team in order to address the medical, nutritional and therapeutic needs of the child and the family. The members of the multi-disciplinary team may include a GP, psychologist, counsellor, psychiatrist and dietitian.

Nutrition counselling is an important part of the overall care of children with eating disorders. People with eating disorders tend to have an excellent knowledge of the calorie content of foods but hold a distorted view of their own nutritional requirements and have unrealistic weight goals. Even after their fears of dietary change have been reduced, sufferers lack the general nutritional knowledge of how to plan and achieve appropriate dietary intakes. This is where individualised advice can be beneficial to the sufferer to help them in their attempt to normalise their eating behaviour.

Dietary advice is based on the *Guidelines for Healthy Eating* from the Department of Health and Children. A system of food 'portions' combined with the concept of the food pyramid, which includes the four main food groups, can be useful tools when devising meal plans. Rigid meal plans which lack variety are generally not beneficial. The aims of the nutritional treatment of eating disorders are to help the individual to:

- Normalise eating behaviour
- Establish regular eating patterns

- Establish normal range of foods eaten
- Reduce the fear of dietary change
- Correct abnormal attitudes towards food and dispel any food myths

Dietary Management of Anorexia Nervosa

The overall goal of treatment is to reverse weight loss and restore good health. Early diagnosis of anorexia nervosa is important as many complications are related to the duration of the illness and age of onset. In a growing child anorexia nervosa can have a significant effect on health in as little as six months. However, in the initial stages of treatment for children and adolescents who are not critically underweight, the focus should be on achieving dietary changes that improve the overall nutritional quality of the diet and eating pattern rather than focusing immediately on weight gain. The aim should be to achieve weight maintenance initially and prevent further weight loss. It is very important when the child is starting to feed again that he or she takes it slowly initially and that small portions of food are eaten at regular times. Sufferers of anorexia nervosa may eat as little as a quarter of their actual needs.

Sample diet history of 15-year-old female with anorexia nervosa

Breakfast	2 strawberry diet yoghurts or 1 banana and plum
Lunch	1 slice brown bread (without butter) and a banana or a wrap with 1 slice of chicken
Dinner	1 chicken breast with large portion of vegetables and ½ boiled potato without butter or gravy

Nutritional Goals

- To achieve normal growth and development for age
- To achieve normal body weight for age and height
- To replenish nutrient stores
- To normalise and promote healthy eating pattern
- To manage weight gain

In most patients with anorexia nervosa, an average weekly weight gain of 0.5kg in out-patient settings and 0.5-1kg in in-patient settings should be an aim of treatment (NICE Guidelines, 2004).

Weight Monitoring

Regular weight checks are necessary as part of the treatment of anorexia nervosa in order to monitor medical risk. Weighing scales vary in accuracy and in order to prevent unnecessary confusion and distress, keep to the same scales, for example GP's scales or home scales. (Bear in mind that weighing scales in the home are rarely accurate.)

At times it may be necessary not to disclose the child's weight to him or her and to try to take the focus off the weight, especially if it has become an obsession. Some parents like to keep a weight chart as a way of monitoring progress. Beware that children may use devious ploys such as hiding stones, mobile phones and mirrors in their pockets to ensure their weight appears greater than it actually is.

- Weight checks should be weekly
- Weighing should be done at the same time of day (ideally before breakfast)

- Children should be weighed with a minimum of clothing, no shoes and with an empty bladder

Dietary Guidelines

- Establish a regular meal pattern i.e. breakfast, lunch and dinner. To sustain weight gain it is necessary to aim for six meals per day, that is three meals and three snacks. This may take several weeks to establish.
- The initial meal plan should involve foods from each of the main food groups to help establish a varied and balanced diet.
- Choose foods that your child prefers to eat.
- Encourage family-centred meals.
- Prevent your child 'filling up' on large quantities of fruit and vegetables. He/she may have got into the routine of eating such a diet and will need to gradually limit their intake to two portions of fruit and two portions of vegetables per day.
- Prevent your child drinking excessive volumes of fluids. Encourage a glass of water (200mls) or other preferred drink with each meal and snack. Limit intake of fizzy drinks. Caffeinated drinks should be drunk in moderation.
- Discuss non-food related issues at the dinner table to take the focus off food i.e. avoid talking about the food problem.
- Allow your child to provide some input into the meal plan, for instance snack suggestions, so that he/she feels some ownership.

- Several vitamin and mineral deficiencies including iron, calcium and zinc have been linked with anorexia nervosa. Fortunately they normalise with re-feeding. Calcium supplements are occasionally recommended if the condition is chronic and there is a risk to the child's bone health.
- If food refusal and/or poor weight gain is a problem some children may benefit from taking nutritional supplements in the form of high calorie sip drinks and/or milkshakes. These supplements need to be prescribed by your doctor and should only be taken under medical supervision.

WHAT A PARENT CAN DO TO HELP

Preparation and Supervision of Meals
It may be necessary and beneficial for the parent to take on the responsibility for preparing and serving all meals and for supervising mealtimes.

Making a Weekly Menu Plan
It can be helpful to have the meals for the day planned in advance to reduce stress and possible tension at mealtimes. It can be a good idea to draw up a weekly menu plan which is jointly agreed by the parent and child, and assign different meals to different days of the week e.g. Monday: chicken curry; Tuesday: spaghetti Bolognese. Once the meal plan is written and agreed it should be made clear that no alterations are to be made to it.

Recording Food Intake

It may be useful to establish an awareness of your child's eating habits by recording what is eaten each day. They should be kept by the parents and not become the focus of the child's attention. These charts can be useful for reviewing at clinic appointments.

Adjusting Your Shopping List

Choose whole milk, full-fat yoghurts, full-fat cheese and avoid buying any 'diet' or low fat products.

Individual portions can be very useful as they reduce the conflict over portion sizes at mealtimes. These include:

- Butter/margarine
- Cheese e.g. cream cheese or slices of cheddar
- Bags of rice
- Pots of custard or puddings

NUTRITIONAL MANAGEMENT OF BULIMIA NERVOSA

Children and adolescents with bulimia nervosa experience episodes of binge-eating, purging and intermittent restricted eating. Large quantities of food, frequently high in carbohydrate or sugar are consumed (approximately 2000-4000 calories per binge episode). Purging behaviours do not completely prevent the utilisation of calories from the binge; on average the sufferer retains 1200 calories from binges.

The binge may be planned or unplanned, but is associated with loss of control over eating. A structured eating plan based around regular meals and snacks should prevent excess hunger and help to normalise eating. In time this should facilitate the return of normal hunger and satiety cues, reduce bingeing and purging behaviours and minimise unwanted weight gain.

Sample diet history of 15-year-old female with bulimia nervosa

Breakfast	Skips breakfast
Mid-morning	Avoids snack
Lunch	Large turkey and cheese bread roll, can of Coke, packet of crisps
Mid-afternoon	2 bars of chocolate and can of Coke
Dinner	Lasagne with garlic bread and chips, glass of Coke and 4 biscuits
Bedtime	2 packets of crisps, 4 biscuits and a glass of Coke

Nutritional Goals

- Maintain weight within normal weight range for height and age
- Minimise weight gain in normal to overweight adolescents
- Normalise and promote healthy eating patterns

Dietary Guidelines

- Establish regular meal pattern. A consistent and disciplined schedule is needed and this may take several weeks to establish.
- Snacks between meals may need to be included as part of the meal plan in order to maintain weight.
- Encourage family-centred meals.
- An agreed snack at bedtime can be helpful as this is the most likely time for binge episodes to occur.
- Discourage dieting/restrictive behaviours.
- Limit exposure to highly palatable (high sugar/

high fat) or known binge foods.

- Foods with a low Glycaemic Index (GI) and/or high fibre content may be helpful as these foods generally pass slowly through the gut and your child feel fuller for longer. Foods which have a low GI include, pasta, porridge, bran-based breakfast cereals, fruit and vegetables, whereas pastries, high-sugar drinks and confectionery have a high GI.

What a Parent Can Do to Help

Strategies to help reduce binge episodes:

- Minimise food stores at home. Avoid purchasing large portion sizes of foods and if possible try to shop day-to-day.
- Avoid purchasing highly palatable foods and having them on display.
- Encourage your child to eat slowly and to put utensils down between bites.
- Place an average serving of food on the plate.

HEALTHY EATING ADVICE

The overall task is to translate nutritional goals into a healthy eating plan. The following guidelines are the basis for a healthy eating plan:

- Include a wide variety of foods and include at least the minimum number of servings from each food group each day. The portion size of foods and rate of progression will vary from one individual to another and the meal plan may take weeks to become established.

- Food should be eaten at least every three to four hours during the day.
- Starchy foods such as pasta, potatoes or rice should be the basis for the main meals. It may be necessary to choose high-fibre varieties if constipation is a problem but fibre intake should not be excessive as may cause bloating and feeling of fullness.
- Aim for a minimum of three to five servings of dairy products each day. A serving is equivalent to 1/2pt milk (200mls)/150g pot yoghurt/1oz cheese. Avoid fat-free varieties.
- It may be useful to work with different types of meat/fish/poultry initially and include a source at lunch and at dinner-time. A portion is about the size of the palm of the hand. If your child is vegetarian, please refer to vegetarian section for alternative advice.
- Enjoy moderate exercise in a social setting but avoid excessive/compulsive exercise to burn calories.

Snacking

Suitable snacks can contribute significantly to your child's overall nutritional intake for the day and help with weight gain. Suitable snack ideas are:

- Small scone
- Pot full-fat yoghurt (150g)
- Fruit or cereal-type bar e.g. fig roll/ Nutrigrain
- Packet peanuts
- Bottle of fruit smoothie made with yoghurt

- Large piece of fruit
- Small bowl cereal with full-fat milk
- Crackers (two) and hummous or peanut butter
- Slice of toast with portion of margarine/butter (restaurant size pre-packaged portions)

Vegetarian Diets

It is not uncommon for adolescents with eating disorders to be vegetarian. If your child decides to follow a vegetarian diet it is important to choose the right variety of foods to provide all the essential nutrients needed for health. Depending on the type of vegetarian diet some nutrients are at particular risk, including calcium, Vitamin B12, Iron, Zinc and Vitamin D.

To ensure nutritional adequacy, it is helpful to consider the four main food groups outlined above. As an alternative to meat the following food groups provide protein, iron and zinc: legumes (peas, beans and lentils); soya-based foods including tofu, nuts and seeds; eggs (if eaten); whole grains

Vegetarian Meal Suggestions

- Vegetable stir-fry with tofu and noodles or rice
- Remove a portion of sauce for Bolognese, casserole, curry or chilli before meat is added. Add beans, lentils, tofu, nuts as alternative protein for the vegetarian portion.
- Mixed bean curry with rice
- Vegetarian quiche
- Vegetable burgers

HEALTHY MEAL PLAN

Variations of this sample meal plan are also suitable and the basic structure can be adapted to suit your child's needs. It may take several weeks before the quantities of foods and the regularity of meals and snacks are achieved. Tea, coffee, water or other drinks are extras to the meal plan. If your child is vegetarian refer to section on vegetarian diet for more ideas

Breakfast	Bowl cereal (40g) with whole milk (200ml) and toast (2 slices) with portion of margarine/ butter per slice (restaurant size pre-packaged portions) and glass of orange juice (with or without fortified calcium) (100ml)
Mid-morning:	Choose from suitable snack list
Lunch	Bread (2 slices) or medium bread roll or large pitta pocket or wrap with portion of margarine/butter per slice and protein filling – ham (1 slice) or chicken (1 slice) or fish (small tin) or eggs (2) or cheese (2 slices) – and salad (1-2 portions) and glass milk (200ml) or yoghurt (150g pot) or fruit smoothie (200ml) or pot custard or pudding
Mid-afternoon	Choose from suitable snack list
Dinner	Potatoes (2 scoops) or 4 heaped tablespoons pasta or rice or couscous and portion of protein (chicken breast or fish fillet or other meat 1—2 thick slices) and vegetables (1-2 portions) and glass milk (200ml) or yoghurt (150g pot) or fruit smoothie (200ml) or pot custard or pudding
Evening	Choose from suitable snack list

Managing Mealtimes

Parents differ in how they manage a young person with an eating disorder. Some will use a firm approach to encourage their child to eat will others have a gentle, relaxed attitude and offer rewards for any food eaten. A common source of conflict in the management of eating disorders is lack of consistency between parents. This can only lead to confusion and tension. Parents need to be able to compromise and devise a management strategy that they are both comfortable with.

Parents may fall into the trap of adopting a particular approach for one or two days and changing tactics if this is unsuccessful. This only serves to delay recovery as improvement is not achievable until the approach is consistent. Parents may need to change their own behaviour and agree to avoid confrontation at the dinner table, for example shouting at children if food is not eaten.

Parents should try to move the focus away from food and on to values such as health and lifetime goals, avoiding taking part in conversations about food, diets, calories and weight. They should:

- Be consistent in their approach
- Avoid making empty promises
- Avoid force feeding
- Avoid using threats
- Avoid making special meals for their child
- Avoid labelling food as 'good', 'bad', 'healthy', 'junk'
- Try to have one family meal together every day
- Limit mealtime to thirty minutes
- Discuss non-food-related topics at the table

- Avoid commenting on the nutritional content of foods

CHILDHOOD OBESITY

There have been major changes in our eating habits over the last few decades; what we eat, where we eat and when we eat. There is no doubt that these changes have contributed to the growing obesity problem in Ireland. Not all children carrying extra pounds are overweight or obese. If you as a parent are worried that their child is putting on too much weight, talk to your GP. He or she can provide a weight assessment, taking into account your child's individual history of growth and development and where your child is on the growth chart. This can help determine if the child's weight is in an unhealthy weight range.

Childhood obesity may arise from genetic and hormonal causes but most excess weight is caused by children eating too much and exercising too little. Many children spend more time watching television, playing computer games and surfing the internet than playing sports or riding their bikes. A recent study found that Irish children eat most of their meals and snacks at home (IUNA, 2005). In view of the escalating problem of obesity among children this is quite a remarkable finding as it highlights that the home environment has a critical influence on children's eating habits and possible risk of developing obesity. Parents have a strong influence over whether or not their child will become overweight or obese as parents play a very important role in developing their child's eating habits and activity preferences.

Until quite recently, childhood obesity was seen as a cosmetic problem. It is now well recognised that childhood obesity may have many serious health consequences which include:

- Diabetes
- Heart disease
- High blood pressure
- High cholesterol
- Asthma
- Psychological consequences, such as low self-esteem, bullying

Recommendations

Childhood obesity is a family issue. One of the best strategies to combat excess weight in children is to improve the diet and exercise levels of the entire family. The whole family should get involved in healthy eating practices which protect the obese child from being singled out and stigmatised at home. Parents should encourage family meals and reduce children's access to high calorie foods and drinks at home and when eating outside the home. Generally the aim is to slow or halt weight gain so the child will grow into his or her body weight over a period of months or years. The methods for maintaining weight or losing weight are the same: the child needs to eat a healthy diet and increase his or her physical activity. Success depends largely on the commitment of the parents.

Healthy Eating

A number of healthy changes can be made to the family diet:

- Eating a wide variety of foods
- Increasing intake of fruit and vegetables
- Reducing intake of high-calorie (high-fat and high-sugar) snack foods
- Using low-fat cooking methods like grilling,

baking, boiling
- Eating more fibre-rich foods like wholemeal breads and whole grain breakfast cereals
- Eating a breakfast every morning
- Eating only at recognised meal and snack times, preferably as a family
- Avoiding eating in front of the television
- Reducing the number of visits to the takeaway

Physical Activity
- Limit sedentary activity, for example TV-viewing, to one to two hours per day.
- Children should aim for one hour of physical activity every day.
- Children should be encouraged to include physical activity in their daily lives, for example walking the dog, walking to and/or home from school, getting off the bus a few stops sooner, taking the stairs instead of the lift or elevator.
- Encourage hobbies that are active.

Weight
Rapid weight loss and strict dieting are not appropriate for growing children who are overweight or obese. The recommended weight loss is 0.5 kg (1lb) per month. In fact, many children who are overweight should in time grow into their weight if they adopt healthy eating habits. Weight checks should be once a week at a maximum; weighing once a month may be more realistic for evaluating progress.

CONCLUSION

Eating disorders and obesity in children are becoming more and more common in Irish society. If a parent has serious concerns about their child's eating behaviour they should seek help immediately. Taking action early and getting the correct advice may improve the child's wellbeing and health in the short and long term. Eating disorders are complex conditions and require expert input from professionals in many disciplines.

Appendix A: Suggested Meal Plans

FEMALE 15 YEARS OLD, DIAGNOSIS: ANOREXIA NERVOSA

Meal	Monday	Tuesday	Wednesday
Breakfast	50g oats + 200ml milk 2 slices brown toast + 2 pats butter 150ml orange juice	50g cornflakes + 200ml milk 2 slices brown toast+2 pats butter 150ml orange juice	50g oats + 200ml milk 2 slices brown toast + 2 pats butter 150ml orange juice
Mid-morning	Fruit yoghurt + handful nuts	Nut yoghurt	Apple + handful nuts
Lunch	2 slices white bread + 2 pats butter, 1 turkey slice, salad Fig roll bar	2 slices white bread + 2 pats butter 8 Cajun prawns, salad Fruit yoghurt	1 bagel + 2 portions cream cheese Nut yoghurt
Mid-afternoon	Handful raisins + fruit yoghurt	Orange	Bag popcorn
Dinner	Grilled breast of chicken 2 medium potatoes broccoli + carrots 200ml fruit smoothie	Stir-fry with breast chicken 1 'boil in bag' rice	Baked fillet of cod 2 scoops potatoes broccoli 200ml milk

| Bedtime | Small packet nuts | Fig roll bar + handful raisins | 1 slice cheese on 1 slice toast |

MALE 15 YEARS OLD, DIAGNOSIS: ANOREXIA NERVOSA

Meal	Monday	Tuesday	Wednesday
Breakfast	50g cornflakes + 200ml milk 2 slices white toast + 2 pats butter 150ml orange juice	2 Weetabix + 200ml milk 2 slices white toast + 2 pats butter 150ml orange juice	50g cornflakes + 200ml milk 2 slices white toast + 2 pats butter 150ml orange juice
Mid-morning	Nutrigrain bar	Nutrigrain bar	Fig roll bar
Lunch	Large roll with 2 pats butter Chicken tikka pieces Fruit yoghurt	Large roll with 2 pats butter Handful grated cheese Fruit yoghurt	4 slices white bread with 2 pats butter 2 slices ham Nut yoghurt
Mid-afternoon	Apple	Banana	Banana
Dinner	6oz fried monkfish 200g mashed potatoes 1/3 plate vegetables 1 scoop ice-cream	6oz roast chicken with gravy 200g mashed potatoes Broccoli and carrots Fruit yoghurt	Stir-fry with breast chicken 200g noodles Mixed vegetables 1 scoop ice-cream
Bedtime	2 biscuits and 200ml milk	Small bowl cereal with milk	2 biscuits and 200ml milk

APPENDIX B: RECOMMENDED DAILY ALLOWANCES (FSAI)

Age	Calcium mg/day	Vit D ug/day	Iron mg/day	Vit C mg/day	Folate ug/day	Vit A ug/day
4-6	800	0-10	9	45	200	400
7-10	800	0-10	10	45	200	500
Girls						
11-14	1200	0-15	14	50	300	600
15-17	1200	0-15	14	60	300	600
Boys						
11-14	1200	0-15	13	50	300	600
15-17	1200	0-15	14	60	300	700

REFERENCES/RESOURCES IN THE AREA OF NUTRITION

American Dietetic Association (ADA). Members of the public can access a position paper on nutrition intervention in the treatment of anorexia, nervosa and other eating disorders. www.eatright.org.

Field et al (2001). 'Peer, Parent and Media Influences on the Development of Weight Concerns and Frequent Dieting among Pre-adolescent and Adolescent Girls and Boys.' *Pediatrics* 107 (1): 54-60.

Irish Nutrition and Dietetic Institute (INDI). www.indi.ie.

Irish Universities Nutrition Alliance (IUNA). *National Children's Food Survey* (2005). www.iuna.net.

National Institute for Clinical Excellence (NICE). Eating Disorders: Quick Reference Guide, 2004. www.nice.org.uk.

Food Safely Authority of Ireland. Recommended Dietary Allowances for Ireland, 1999. www.fsai.ie.

Department of Health and Children. *The Irish Health Behaviour in School-Aged Children Study* (HBSC), 2006. www.doh.ie

Nutrition Booklets

Health Service Executive. *Guide to Daily Healthy Food Choices.* www.healthinfo.ie.

Irish Nutrition and Dietetic Institute (INDI). *Guide to Vegetarian Eating*.www.indi.ie.

5

My Journey

Áine Crowley, Artist

There is not a day that goes by that I do not think about the girl I was and the girl I have become. I do not believe in self pity but there are times that I feel sorry for that girl, I mean me. Sometimes I find it hard to believe that it was me who was so compulsive, obsessive, selfish and scared. I know why I ended up with an eating disorder but I still wonder how.

On 14 August 2002, I was diagnosed with anorexia nervosa by my psychiatrist. I remember feeling like laughing, I was in total denial. In my eyes, life could not have been any better. Although I have always been a big worrier and there were a lot of things happening in my life that I could not control, I chose to put them in the back of my mind. As my wardrobe grew in clothes that were too big for me, my mental happiness deteriorated, the silliest things started to eat away at me…the dirty cup left out, the colour run in my whites…how could people be so careless! The comments went from, 'Áine, you look fab,' to 'Áine, what's wrong?' My family confronted me about my weight loss numerous times, I remember thinking they were overreacting and nobody could make me gain weight, especially when there was nothing wrong. I was happy.

When I look back now I wish someone had put a camera on me for a day. My temper was short; I was totally erratic; I was a mental wreck; The smallest things made me cry, the important things flew straight over my head. Physically I was ugly, exactly the opposite of what I thought I was achieving, I was no longer a woman, not even a child. My bones jutted out in places I did not think were possible. At the time I just saw flesh and too much of it. Now I think: how could a mind deceive someone so much and how did I become so obsessed with my appearance?

It was the end of my first year in art college that I began to get sick. I remember it was a time when I had begun to put a lot of pressure on myself, to prove to myself and others that I was not wasting my time in art college. There was a lot of other things going on in my life at the time, stuff that I had no control over. I clearly remember the moment I made the conscious decision to prove myself. What I did not realise was that it was a decision that I would lose control over and regret for the rest of my life. I never actually decided to stop eating but I did promise myself I would work harder at college, so much so that I began to miss meals, which in turn led to my losing a few pounds. When I returned to college after the Easter holidays one of my friends pulled me aside and asked what was going on. I knew I had lost a few pounds but felt her reaction was a bit extreme. After all it was only two weeks since we had last met. That was March 2002.

26 March 02
Had 2 talk to someone about what's going on in my mind. I feel so out of my depth.

By the end of April/start of May it was obvious to everyone but me what was going on. I did not see it but the weight was falling off me at an alarming rate. I knew my body felt different and there were different things happening inside me. I never once related these feelings to the fact I was living on a Tracker bar.

29 April 02
Really weird feeling in my tummy, like a twitch.

However, I had this overwhelming feeling of control over everything, from my college work, which had become my drug, to my happiness. I do believe at that time I was very happy I had an amazing boyfriend and I was doing really well in college but as the weeks went on I was changing. I remember my father ringing me and saying he was worried about me and thought I was working too hard and that I looked wrecked. At this stage my family were well aware of what was wrong. In a way I remember being glad that someone was noticing that something was wrong, *what* I don't know. By mid June things were getting out of control. I always denied making myself sick. I think that was because I believed they were the actions of someone with an eating disorder.

18 June 02
It had 2 come up; sorry!

Even in my diary I could not admit it properly. It is only in the last couple of years since I've gotten better that I can admit I had a touch of bulimia too. Actually typing it now feels weird, I think it is the first time I have seen it in words…the same for taking laxatives!

At this stage of my eating disorder I began to lose interest in everything except food.

I was becoming sneaky with food, preparing it and then throwing it away...

28 June 02
Dad was messing with me about food, completely lost it with him, felt so angry. How dare he pass such comments. Every 1 is on2 me and won't leave it.

29 June 02
Dad said it 2 me about what happened yesterday, he reckons my reaction 2wards what he said was enough 2 convince him that there was something up.... I convinced him otherwise.

3 July 2
Mum's on2 me about my weight!!!

I think this was the first time I ever got aggressive about food. I was down in the shop with Dad (we owned a supermarket at the time) and I was very hungry. I knew I was not going to eat the food I was preparing, I was doing it for show. Dad passed a comment: 'God, Áine you must be very hungry!' and I lost it with him. I threw the spoon at the aluminium plate and got so frustrated and angry. The heat and sweat were unbearable, the look on my father's face was heartbreaking but all I could think was how dare he comment. I wrapped the plate of food, left the shop and dumped it in a bin near my house. I was so deceitful at this stage that I had hidden a second aluminium under the one that was piled high with food to bring home so everyone would think I had eaten.

The reason I am using my diary entries is because these are the words that frightened me into coming to my senses. I will never be able to tell the story of my eating disorder the way my diary can. To this day I get a shiver through my body when I read it. The mind of a person with an eating disorder is very deceitful. It is probably one of the hardest things to explain to someone and the most difficult thing to understand. An eating disorder is a death sentence: it does not just eat at the body but the mind too. The mind is very powerful and much stronger than the heart. Everyday I promised myself I would change but I could not. My diary is quite raw, at times I think almost crazy. To this day I find it impossible to believe it is mine and that it was my mind and hand that wrote those words. I think if I were to write this piece in my own words today it would be wrapped in cotton wool. I am embarrassed but not ashamed by a lot of things that went on in my head and how I was but what good would this piece be if I was not honest…to myself and to those reading it. It is very hard to remember that the person is not the only one making the decisions – the eating disorder makes them too.

15 July 02
(deliberately left the sentences overflow for effect…)
Called down 2 dad after work; he was really silent with me but then got
really upset and started crying; I almost admitted something but the words
couldn't and wouldn't come out of my mouth. I know there's something wrong
but I don't know what, I know I'm not myself. He said my face is getting

older he thinks I'm losing 2 much weight. He was so upset it scared me, he told me I'm 2 precious 2 b doing this 2 myself. I promised things would change. It's killing me 2 see the both of them like this, I know mum is saying nothing cause she knows I'll blow up with her. I can't help what's going on, I'm full of energy and life but inside I know there's something wrong, maybe I do need help but I really don't want it. I feel like I'm losing independence with every 1 watching me.

29 July 02
Dad was on2 me again today, he thinks
I'm working 2 hard…. I just need 2 be
left alone. He said I'm beginning 2 remind him of the day I was born, 'small', 'boney' and 'frail'. He said he keeps thinking of how mum used 2 be scared of me playing with the lads in case they'd break me – I can't help this…

31 July 02
Mum and dad got stuff on eating disorders in the post; dad said to me there was something in their room that he wanted me to read. I found it and read it. All the booklets inform you is that everyone fits the criteria of a person with an eating disorder. There is one thing that kinda made me stop and think…one's obsession with making food for others…

2 August 02
Mum and dad have been really silent with me…it's really uncomfortable.

3 August 02
They told me 2day I have 2 go and see a specialist when I get back from holidays. I didn't say anything or ask any questions, I don't want 2 argue with them any more, anyway it's the last thing I want 2 be

thinking about on holidays.

5 August 02

Having a great time but so tired.

13 August 02

Things were really weird when I got back
2night didn't know what 2 say or how 2 act, scared about 2morrow.

14 August 02

I've been dreading this day. Went 2 the specialist. It was horrible and undermining. She said I'm underweight, she said I have anorexia. It's ridiculous, my clothes may be a little bigger but I'm not 2 thin, I've been working hard and I feel good. I mightn't be allowed 2 go back 2 college, why…what good will that do me. I don't know what 2 do I have no 1 2 talk 2, how could anybody understand, I feel like a bold child being scolded for something I didn't do. I know every 1 has been saying I've lost weight but that's them being concerned, that's what friends do. 1 has a concern and says it 2 another and then every 1 gets all concerned. I don't want 2 put on weight, I don't want 2 feel so alienated. I can't even answer the phone…Everyone is texting and ringing 2 find out about my holidays, I have no 1. What am I going 2 do?
Thanks for your reassuring words Joe, you were the only 1 I could bear in my room. It's weird the way the table turns, no 1 ever knew I'd be going through this…we're very much alike, you're an amazing brother.

When I read this part of my diary I realise how confused and erratic I was, I could not think straight; everything that came into my mind was negative and a contradiction. It frightens me to think that I could not see around this. All my thoughts and words were such opposites. Did I ever think of re-reading what I had written. Would that have worked? Would that have made me think twice and see how insane my thoughts were?

16 August 02

I can't even face the sight of food. Ye have made it an issue now. I'm not stupid – I can see ye checking the brown bread 2 see if I've eaten anything…just ask me. I can hear ye talking about me, I'm not fucking deaf…please, please stop it's all 2 silly, I know what I'm like…I'll do exactly what ye are expecting…Not eat…nothing!!!!

17 August 02

Every 1 is really beginning 2 annoy me…all the questions. Mum I swear I meant what I said 2night I will work at this, I know my humour has been really bad the last few days and I'm sorry.

Almost admitted the whole psychiatrist thing 2 a friend…but there was no point. I know he's worried, but telling him would only make him think there is something wrong; I assured him everything is being taken care of. But I'm not 2 sure if it is, I'm feeling really low.

19 August 02

Had the psychiatrist again 2day. Lost more weight since Wednesday. She said if I continue 2 lose weight I'll be taken out of work. This whole thing is getting really frustrating, I can't even choose from a menu, I get so panicky, almost angry.

20 August 02

My stomach is so sore, the pains are unreal. Maybe it's what I ate yesterday!

21 August 02

I feel so frustrated, I can't do anything in front of people, I'm struggling 2 follow a natural instinct, eating; I can't even use a knife and fork. I feel completely stupid, I don't know how 2 act around any1. I know that some1's always watching me 2 make sure I'm OK. Every time I leave the room every1 has a little conferring session…'How much did she this, how much did she that'…just ask me !I know what's going on remember it's meant 2 be me whose causing all this grief, and believe me I know how much I've eaten, how can I forget now.

To this day I wonder when I became so obsessed with food and my weight. I went from being happy and confident to so low and obsessed. Maybe being told by a stranger was what made it all hit home. When I left the psychiatrist's office that first day, I became aware and completely obsessed with what I had come to believe was a way of living.

From the day I was told I was anorexic, I began to struggle with natural things. Holding and choosing from a menu became unbearable. Even though I wanted the food I could not get the words out of my mouth. I was constantly living with a ball of tension in my stomach and had myself believing that this was my body telling me I did not need the food. I found it impossible to use a knife and fork. If the food fell off the fork I would get so frustrated and panic. The feelings and emotions I would go through were impossible to explain, let alone understand. If someone other than my family were in the house while I was eating I would give up; sometimes throwing in the towel was a good feeling; other times I realised it was insane. My parents' lives revolved around making sure I had my few pieces of brown bread; My mother would drive the length and breadth of the country looking for the brown bread I would eat. If she could not get it, I simply would not eat.

23 August 02

Not sleeping 2 well, keep waking and having major cravings 4 orange juice.

My tummy is like a ball of tension. I feel so wound up, snapped at Rob this evening, I knew straight away I was out of order but I couldn't bring myself 2 say sorry...Sorry Rob I'm being so selfish.

24 August 02

I don't think I can do this any more, I feel like crying the whole time, and people keep on making comments that are making me feel really uncomfortable.

Throughout my eating disorder I found it impossible to apologise to my family for my outbursts and bad manner. The first time I said sorry to anyone was after I read my diary. I would shout and roar at my brothers over simple things. One of my brothers, Robert, would put himself in the firing line so I would lose my temper on him rather than my Mum. I am lucky I had such an understanding family. I am not too sure if I could have tolerated what they did.

26 August 02

Back at the psychiatrist again 2day. I'm losing weight drastically fast, 5 more pounds since Monday.

I've been pulled out of work. I swear I've been trying, what are people going 2 say now? Of course they're going 2 think there's something wrong with me, they as good as want me bed- bound. Mel is home and I don't know how she feels or even if she thinks I look unwell, I can't even talk 2 her and that's not like me, we never stop talking when she comes home.

27 August 02

Completely freaked out 2day, nearly smashed the plate of food, I just couldn't face it. I really did try! You'd swear I was being challenged by a monster, I went 4 a walk instead, visited grandad's grave. All I could do was cry. I feel so frustrated how can such a thing be after taking over my life? Before I started going 2 the psychiatrist things were easy and carefree. Mel came up 2 the grave 2 me. I don't know what I'd do without her, she helped me 2 find the funny side of this thing, I guess if you can't laugh at yourself who can you laugh at. That's what I love about her, there's always a brighter side, so happy she found me. We had a really good chat, think she's the first person I've totally opened up 2. She seemed 2 understand the things I couldn't, she made me realise I'm not alone. Thanks Mel.

When I was pulled out of work I felt like a complete failure. Things seemed to be getting worse for me. I was totally paranoid as to what people would think and say: 'Is she in hospital?' Now I wonder, because I was so paranoid about what people thought, I obviously must have known that there was something wrong. My attitude towards food became more aggressive. Food became the biggest challenge, and I was physically battling with it the whole time. At the end of the summer of 2002, Mel, one of my closest friends, came over from England to see me and when I met her at the airport I thought her tears were tears of happiness. Later I realised how upset she was to see what I had done to myself.

Mel was the person who brought out the lighter side of me again. She helped me see the funny side of things. If I continued to dwell on the bad it was going to continue to eat at me. Somehow in my head, making light of it helped me to talk about it. Mel helped me set little guidelines and new rules. I set certain times to eat and had to eat at those times. At first these new rules did not exactly sort the problem but I knew they could not be broken. In time I began looking forward to my meals.

28 August 02

I'm going 2 put yesterday behind me and make a new start. It's weird really, I feel comfortable with certain foods and then there are others I can't bear to think of. Things that are small and light seem safer and less daunting, like peanuts. I know they are fattening but they are easier than an apple to eat.

I've decided 2day I was going 2 set myself a certain time 2 eat my dinner…5 o'clock, but when the time came I felt so tense and my mood completely changed. Afterwards I could feel myself getting more and more worked up and couldn't bear the company of others. I feel so guilty. Mum is putting up with so much. I wish I never went 2 the psychiatrist, I wouldn't be feeling like this now. Since I've started going 2 her I have all these fears and silly notions and every 1 is all concerned about me which is making me more and more worked up.

I can't bear the company of any1.

3 September 02

The psychiatrist reckons a lot of this is down 2 the pressure I put on myself, I don't know about that though, every 1 needs pressure.

6 September 02

First time in a long time I have felt real hunger pains and felt pretty much OK after my dinner. However, it's funny when I see how worked up I get about my small plate of food and then I look at every 1 else's plate. What kind of reaction would I have if their plate was mine?

9 September 02

Back to college 2 day, couldn't eat this morning with nerves, 2nd year sounds pretty deadly though.

Got really weak in the evening. All of the year were packed in 2 a room, felt so awkward. There was no air, thought I was going 2 faint, I could hear and feel my heart thumping, couldn't hear or see properly. It really scared me but the minute I got home I was grand again. Didn't feel like eating anything. 2 wrecked.

11 September 02
Can't stop crying.

13 September 02
Back 2 the psychiatrist 2 day, lost weight again. She said I'll end up in hospital if I'm not careful.

19 September 02
Can't
Sleep anymore.

20 September 02
Got on well with the psychiatrist 2day, gained 1 pound....... Every 1 was so happy!!!!
Met up with the girls. Didn't stay out for long. Felt really weird and didn't know what 2 say 2 them. I know they know there's something up, Besides that I felt so paranoid, I felt like every1 was looking at
Me. Even the way people were talking 2 me was so condescending, I felt so little, I actually felt like I was a sick person.

27 September 02
Psychiatrist again 2 day, lost weight again. She wants 2 put me on anti-depressants. She said my body is beginning 2 eat my muscles and that if I'm not careful my heart will become weak. I just don't seem 2 be getting this whole scare tactic thing, sometimes I actually feel like laughing...It's like telling a child 2 be good or you can't go 2 your

friends house…a threat!!!!!!!

Going back to college was a great feeling. I truly believed that at college I was Áine and at home I was the sick person. However, it was at college that I began to experience panic attacks and serious weaknesses. No matter how weak I felt, I always relied on someone else to make sure I was OK. I was back in the same city as my boyfriend. He made me look at the brighter side and was amazing to put up with me. He would try to cook different foods for me which I would refuse to eat but he never gave up. However, having someone to rely on was not always a good thing. If he was calling he would look after me; if he was not calling, would I look after myself? That was not right for me or fair on him.

28 September 02
Had to start the anti-depressants. Had no choice, really don't want 2 take them, 2 many people depend on them and my personality is addictive enough but my choice was hospital or the tablets…It really wasn't fair.. I know what is not good 4 me. The psychiatrist reckons I have 2 deal with the depression be 4 I can deal with my other issue, I'm only depressed because I feel suffocated. There's always something.

29 September 02
Woke up this morning. My heart was racing. I was shaking, frozen cold and sweating, couldn't breathe properly, I have never been so scared. Mum called my GP. They think the dosage is 2 high 4 my body so I've been taken off the anti-depressants. Well, at least now I have a reason as 2 why I shouldn't be put back on them. It's almost a blessing in disguise.
Completely doped all day but insisted I go back 2 County Limerick, I'm not weak!

30 September 02
My body has come out in a rash and my chest really hurts. I'm actually petrified. Had 2 get the girls 2 take me 2 the college GP. He was so clueless. He kept going on about how dangerous my problem is, Jesus don't I know? I'm living with it. I just wanted him 2 check my heart. I'm actually convinced my heart is giving in. My whole chest hurts and it won't stop pounding. I'm scared it's going 2 stop. Stupid fucking anti-depressants have fucked me up. I was being independent I didn't need any1 2 nurse me and now Rob has 2 drive up 2 Limerick and take me back home. I look weak, exactly what they want me 2 think.

3 October 02
It's been 5 days since I took the 1 single anti-depressant and I'm just about feeling normal. Mum and Dad have been really good 2 me. Got a load of college work done.

4 October 02
Back 2 the psychiatrist, my weight hasn't budged, considering what happened last week. Don't have 2 take the anti-depressants any more.

11 October 02
Gained 1 pound
Can't handle being around any1.

5 November 02
Feel really shitty, don't want 2 feel like this.
Dreading the thought of Xmas.

6 November 02
Feel like I've been running full force against a wall. It's so much easier

2 stay in bed and ignore what's going on.
I want things 2 go back to normal.

7 November 02
I feel like this whole thing is about some1 else. It's so easy 2 talk in the 2nd person and separate myself from it.

8 November 02
No more lies. I told the psychiatrist everything today. My body is doing something I don't understand any more. Before it was nothing, now I'm completely obsessed.
I've been put on St Johns Wort, I know I'm completely unhappy and at least these tablets are natural. I don't want 2 admit that I'm depressed but I am miserable.
I don't understand what's going on, it's like I have no control over anything anymore. Even my health isn't in my hands, I can't control what I do in regards 2 it. I just have this instant reaction that seems 2 be doing me more bad than good.
I can't expect any1 2 understand what's going on cause I surely don't.

10 November 02
I feel so down.

16 November 02
Had the psychiatrist yesterday, lost weight again?

I'm so moody it's unreal; I'm being so horrible and snappy towards my family and they're saying nothing. I don't even realise how snappy I'm being until afterwards and I still can't bring myself to apologise.
I'm finding everything so hard at the moment.

22 November 02
Put on weight.

25 November 02
Got so weak 2day thought I was going 2 pass out. What scares me the most is that I'm not doing anything 2 stop the weaknesses.

It took me a long time to realise that I was the one out of control and people were only trying to help. I began to realise I was tired of being so angry, paranoid, obsessed and weak. Taking the anti-depressants was a blessing in disguise. Although I had a bad reaction to them, they made me realise how weak I was. I think I finally realised I was sick and desperately needed help. I was not doing anything to help myself and I was tired of feeling like a child. Realising and accepting that was only one step.

29 November 02
Had the psychiatrist again 2day. It was so intense and direct. She probably said everything I didn't want 2 hear. My boyfriend came too, I have been really lucky with him. He has been so good to me and puts up with so much and always keeps a smile on my face. I would be lost without him.
I'm still the same weight. I was back in August and she's on about hospital again…My progress is 2 slow and my body is still in danger…
She mentioned how I've begun 2 reject people and push affection away…I didn't think I was doing that but the more I think about it…it's so true.
She also said that I get very aggressive when I'm asked about food. I thought that was funny but couldn't believe how tough and up straight she was with him there.

6 December 02
Lost again.

16 December 02
The pains in my stomach are unreal, it's like a ball of heat...The psychiatrist reckons it might be an ulcer...what next?

18 December 02
Went 2 my GP 2day. It's an ulcer all right.
Its hard 2 believe I have caused all this pain on my body, yet it doesn't seem 2 be stopping me.

25 December 02
Christmas Day!
As much as I love Christmas I've been dreading this day 4 the last couple of months, but it was a great day. No shitty tension and my form was great.
Every1 had a wonderful day. For the first time in a long time it was like every 1 was totally carefree.

11 January 03
I have totally separated myself from my problem; I can't control any of this if I can't trust myself.

4 February 03
Almost defeated!
I can't even trust what I see when I look at myself. I'm told it's all in my head, I'm deceiving myself...nobody else, but how can that be? I know what I see. I feel like people are playing mind games with me.

25 February 03
So exhausted.

28 February 03
I'm so unhappy 2day. Couldn't get the words out of my mouth, had the psychiatrist, gained, just felt numb.

13 March 03
Broke up with Sam, it had to happen.
Everything seems 2 be lost 2 my illness, Everything is such an effort!

14 March 03
Had the psychiatrist 2day, I was totally distraught. I feel so hysterical. Poor mum.
I've made myself a promise. No more taking, I'm fighting; I'm fighting this...no more walking in old shoes!

16 March 03
It has taken something stupid 2 make me realise it's all over.

As the months went on I began to struggle more and more. I had forgotten what it was to be happy. When I broke up with Sam. I think I realised how much I was losing to my illness. I had depended on him to keep me safe, something no one could do but me. It had all got too much for him. He was carrying my burden and fighting a losing battle too. I could see how I had drained him. He was a fun-loving person and I had sucked that out of him. He could not do anything to help me any more. I was so small he lived in fear of hurting me emotionally and physically. Breaking up with someone who was so important to me hit me in a strange way. It made me more determined to get better, to take care of myself and prove that I was able. However, being alone hit at the weirdest times. Something small would make me cry and make me realise how alone I was and how much I missed having someone. I did not want to be alone forever.

19 March 03
It's me and the TV. Everything I'm doing 2 preoccupy myself is happening 2 fast, Silly things are making me realise what's going on.
It's funny the way people think my form has picked up…if only.
No more dwelling on the past. Life goes on. Maybe things do happen 4 the best.

20 March 03
Why can't I feel what is happening? I just feel alone in my own bubble.
'Gained.'

1 April 03
The penny has dropped. I'm so unhappy and emotional, I was on 2 much of a high. It had 2 come 2 an end.

4 April 03
Lost weight again.

19 April 03
21st birthday
What an amazing night!
What an incredible family!

2 May 03
Gained. Don't feel 2 bad. 8 pebbles, so life can be somewhat normal.

When I reached eight stone I was somewhat relieved to be at a normal weight. However, eight stone was a safety net. How would I deal with gaining more. The smallest things made me feel great, like being able to do a few hours work. I began to feel like Áine again. I still had the somewhat schizophrenic mind of wanting to gain weight and happiness but also knew that this would depress me to hell. What I knew was best for myself was hard to get my head around.

16 May 03
2up, feeling so scared. I feel like I'm losing control. Maybe it's a good thing but I don't like this feeling either.

23 May 03
Neither up nor down, but I feel like I'm gaining some bit of independence. Allowed 2 do a few hours work.

4 June 03
Don't feel 2 positive about myself, I feel like life is going nowhere. I feel that all my decisions have been taken away from me. How does 1 find themselves if they're not given the opportunity 2 do so.

It was around this time that I began to think beyond my eating disorder. Instead of being preoccupied with what was going on with my body, I began to want more for me. I wanted something to look forward to. In saying that the roller coaster was far from over.

7 June 03
I feel like I'm walking in circles.

11 June 03
I needed something...a step forward...you were privileged. First time eating with someone different, choosing off a menu and eating out properly. Thank you 4 making that step so easy...I feel so proud.

It is crazy how scared and proud I felt the first time I ate in a restaurant. It was one of the many little things I thought would be impossible to get through. Whoever would have thought that eating out and choosing from a menu would be so hard for someone? It still shocks me to this day how strong those memories are. It even shocks me to think that those natural activities were ruling my life. I remember that evening I played with the food most of the time and only ate about four spoonfuls. I ordered what I would have eaten in the past, fried rice and sweet and sour sauce. It was easy and safe. I knew I could have gotten out of the situation but I knew that would have been more embarrassing and passing out with the hunger was not something I wanted to happen. I knew deep inside I needed food and I could not act up with this person.

16 June 03
I feel like I have nothing 2 keep me going, nothing 2 look 4ward 2.

27 June 03
8 stone has hit me hard, I've gotten here without trying and I'm so unhappy; I shouldn't feel like this.
I'm scared it's out of control, I don't feel happiness. Nothing should take over some1 especially if they're determined 2 defeat it. I don't think I'm

ready for this. I'm stuck in a deadlock and feel I lack my control. I feel my confidence has gained but with that comes another form of gain that I don't want...since when did this become about gaining?

I don't seem 2 have the control over the only thing I could control. Being less than 8 stone meant I was safe...more of a mental safe. I want my thoughts back.

I would give anything if someone could explain how someone's mind can act like this. Underneath it all I knew what had to be done in order to be happy again, I felt the benefits of gaining weight but I was also in total denial, I still found it mentally hard to deal with my new body, the same body that was making me happy.

10 July 03

I know why I ended up like this. Routine got the better of me, so did the lack of personal control. Instead of fixing all this I took it 2 an extreme.

11 November 03

So mixed up, with both my body and mind. I want 2 feel normal, I'm sick of the pains in my stomach and I'm so sick of worrying about nothing.

I swear I have been trying, but sometimes it gets 2 hard, I'm sick of the constant aggravation I have with myself. I find it so hard 2 imagine myself living like every1 else. What goes in, goes outwards or stays a secret..

Why is everything so difficult? Everyday tasks are challenging and I can't seem 2 do anything 2 make this easier. I feel like I'm 2 different people.

It'd be almost funny if I could make sense of myself.

17 November 03
Mum rang 2day. Couldn't stop crying. Sick of the gripping pains, sick of the constant fear of myself.

30 December 03
Really happy with all the compliments. Every1 is telling me how good I look. I'm actually really proud of myself, which is good. Right!
But these proud feelings kinda scare me 2.

16 January 04
Had the psychiatrist 2day. Gained, Feel so out of control, I'm not eating enough 2 be gaining. You keep saying that the body holds on2 everything when it's not getting enough...and it'll balance itself out when I begin 2 feed it...I wish I could believe that.

6 February 04
Lost weight.

As time went on I began to indulge in my eating disorder and use my experience to help people understand what it is about and how it feels to suffer. In my third year of art college my work was about my guardian angel, but it was the words and the work of a fellow student that made me realise that I was hiding what I was trying to say. I was suffering and alone; my eating disorder had become me.

From the day I decided to confront my problem in my art, my attitude changed. I found my own personal therapy. As I begun to open up and use my negative thoughts in a more positive manner, I began to find Áine, the girl who enjoyed life and people. It was not as straightforward as that, though. Every day was a challenge and I still had a lot of ups and downs. Every day I worked with my eating disorder in my art and every day became a day full of tears. However it became a new sense of addiction. I tried to portray my problem in my art and I began to live by what I was saying in my work. My art became my visual statement to live. Unknown to myself, I began to talk about my problem; my art became the third person. Through it I began to see what others saw. As I pushed my creativity I became the fly on the wall and begun to understand the emotions I was feeling, the pain and isolation I was causing myself and my family. My eating disorder did not began as a bid to achieve the perfect body but as bid to gain control. It was like another person in my life!

25 February 04
It all came 2 me 2day. I've been hiding behind so many things and could never find clarity in my art. The clarity is behind my fears. I'm going 2 work with my feelings in my art, I may shock a lot of people but it's not something they don't know already. I'm taking control of my eating disorder, I'm going 2 feed off it instead of it feeding off me. I'm going 2 take back something it has taken off me…My thoughts and my ability 2 express.

27 February 04
The ultimate clarity
I have spent 2 long hiding behind things and always avoiding the truth. Too scared 2 face things, my ED was my way of protecting myself but it has isolated me. I'm ready 2 do this. I need 2 be clear, I want people 2 understand what this is about and what it's not about.

5 March 04
The psychiatrist is really happy with me and I feel excellent. I told her

what I was going doing with my art. She was happy 4 me; she saw it as my own therapy. Of course I still have all my insecurities but I want 2 fight them, every1 doubts themselves. Only I'm an extremist.

9 March 04
As strong as I want 2 be I feel so tired and worn out. Everything is making me cry, I've been working really hard both with myself and my college work, maybe everything is 2 close 2 my heart. Maybe I can't handle taking this on 24 hours a day, but I have 2 be tough. It's always on my mind anyway so why not push the negative energy and make it positive.

29 March 04
No more St John's Wort.

21 May 04
Felt so emotional, at the psychiatrist's 2day, couldn't stop crying.

25 May 04
This journey has paid off.
I've successfully gained something from my eating disorder. Got my end of year results. Got a great result!!! I spoke through my art, maybe it's 1 thing I can thank my eating disorder for.

1 July 04
Back at the psychiatrist, got on really well, she's really happy with me.

Taking on my eating disorder in my work was a big step and could have backlashed easily. There were so many times that everything got too much for me but the pride I had in my work was unreal. No one could tell me it was right or wrong. But it was something I had complete control over.

In the summer of 2004 I went to London to see Mel for a week and ended up staying there for the whole summer. Being away from everything gave me the chance to make the next step in taking control of my life. Knowing that I would not be seeing the psychiatrist did scare me. I had no one to tell me that what I was feeling was OK. For the next couple of weeks I had to learn to deal with myself or go back home. In London I was just me. I think when I was at home where people knew my history I was always holding back, and sometimes my insecurities were my securities. During my time with Mel in London, I made a trip into London by myself. It was the first time in a long time that I was on my own for a day. I felt like a child. It was great. I spent the day visiting galleries and buying art books. When I felt hungry I got myself a latte and salad and sat on the balcony of the Tate Gallery and ate my first, self chosen, self bought meal *alone* looking over the Thames, smiling!

19 July 04
Off 2 London.

29 July 04
Getting on great, having a ball, so good 2 get away 4m familiar surroundings. Stomach is a bit sore.

1 August 04
Such a weird week, really happy with myself, felt so good doing stuff I normally wouldn't do.

16 August 04
4 the first time in a long time I've met Áine, being away 4m what

reminds me of my past has done me the world of good. I've learnt 2 enjoy my own company. Food has been the last thing on my mind and I'm actually enjoying it without thinking. Feeling sorry 4 myself seems a thing of the past. I've stopped thinking of petty things, I can feel myself responding 2 my body's wants, something I would normally never do, what was unnatural 2 me feels natural. The overwhelming feeling of guilt is lifting; eating seems like a distant problem. I'm beginning 2 do things that I would normally never do at home. Being a stranger feels amazing, no body knows anything about me, I don't feel uncomfortable in my own skin, I'm enjoying being me, I can't recall the last time I felt like this. I'm just the girl with the name every1 can't pronounce, not the 1 who has/had an ED.

My attitude has changed, I feel so motivated. Although I hate people associating me with my problem, I'm not ashamed of it either. I want 2 be noticed 4 the right reasons, not 4 my appearance. I want 2 better myself and achieve more, I want 2 move on. My independence makes me a stronger person. I know if I depend on people I'll give up trying, I need my freedom. I fall in2 ruts that I can't come out of, I let my decisions be taken away 4m me because I believe people know better. I have 2 continue being positive 4 myself, I'm not doing this 4 any1 else but me.

13 August 04
Going home 2day…not ready.

5 September 04
Back to college.

The first time I read my diary was for a piece I decided to do for my degree end-of-year show. I always kept a diary for downloading. Reading the diary was like revisiting the mind that brought me to breaking point. To this day, I truly believe that my diaries were a big factor to me getting my life back on track. I never realised what was going on, how long it had been going on for and how low things had gotten. Reading them made me realise a lot. For one, no matter how hard or low things got I would never let it happen to me again.

Comments like, 'I feel so low', 'I've eaten too much' – to this day I cannot believe that I used such words towards myself.

10 September 04
Had the psychiatrist 2day. Its been a while since I was last with her. Felt pretty good about myself, she was really happy with my attitude 'Held my own'.

8 October 04
Had the psychiatrist 2day, no weighing, but she's really happy with me. She spoke about how far I have come…sometimes I don't even look at it that way though, I know my priorities are in a better place, I care more about realistic things now!!

16 October 04
Feel so weak, my legs are like jelly.

19 October 04
Such a horrible day, I knew the minute I woke up this morning there was no point of getting out of bed. I felt so negative, I couldn't even eat, although I was hungry, just like before.

20 October 04
Still feel horrible, ate a little. Since the start of the summer I know that I

look different but its 4 the best…I look better, I feel better, I have buckets of energy, I can do things without worrying that I'm going 2 pass out. Mentally things are clearer but these insecurities keep consuming me.

No matter how positive I was there were always low days, and sometimes I feared that those days would get the better of me. At times, I wondered was it so right to feel so good and sometimes I was happy to be down. One could never predict what way I would wake up, but I did know the mood I woke up with was staying around for at least a day. Deep down inside I knew I wanted to be happy.

2 November 04
Really good form.

5 November 04
At the psychiatrist 2day. I feel so horrible, but she's really happy with my progress. I feel guilty for feeling like this. These feelings should be behind me. I try 2 ignore them. Sometimes I just 4get them, other times I can't.

22 November 04
Feel great in every way.

3 December 04
At the psychiatrist 2day, got on well. Not seeing her again 4 another 3 months, feels weird.

7 December 04
Feel pretty good!

6 January 05

I doubt my own will, I'll never be able 2 let this go. I feel weak 4m the control you gave me. I have fought the destructive willpower it gave me. I hate its company cause it takes my company away from me. I know I'll never entirely let it go, but at least I've fed off it 2.

10 January 05

I will not doubt myself.

When I read these pieces I find it so hard to believe that it was I who thought the whole world was against her. It took until November 2002 for me to realise that it wasn't my psychiatrist who was causing all these feelings. She was the one who made me realise that I had to deal with them. She was tough on me, gave it to me as it was; there are times I thought she was reading my mind. That first appointment that my parents made with the psychiatrist was my life-line, I always wonder why did I get into the car if I didn't want to go, I think underneath it all I knew I wasn't living a normal life and knew I needed help. The first time I gained weight was like I had won the lotto. All my family were so happy and a part of me was happy for them but gaining a pound was like losing a pound of control.

I continued to see the psychiatrist until the summer of 2006. Although I was in full health for the last year or so, seeing her gave me a sense of security. My sessions were not full of tears or insecurities anymore. If anything I would have the odd moan. My last session was a great feeling but also very difficult. I think I feared that if I ever went downhill I would not have the guts to look for help. However, underneath it all I knew I would not go down that road again. I remember the psychiatrist closing my file and saying how happy she was to be putting closure on it.

My eating disorder is with me to this day but in a positive way now. There is not a week that goes by that I do not think of what my family went through or how lucky I was to have such amazing family and friends. I am just like any other girl now. I still have insecurities – who doesn't? Someone once said to my brother Robert that gaining weight for me was like someone else trying to lose weight. Either way it is was a battle.

6

Life is What You Make It...

Bríd Ní Dheá

In a world of constant competitiveness and chaos many people live their lives striving to be the best that they can and to be accepted by society. Today people are so much more superficial and materialistic and the world seems to revolve around this notion that in order to reach success you need to be accepted by others. We all think that we are normal and like everyone else but what is normality? This is a major issue for many in today's world as we all strive to be successful but also live a normal life.

So what is 'normal' in this ever-changing society? Dictionaries state that it is …' serving to establish a standard' or 'conforming to the standard or the common type; usual; not abnormal; regular; natural'. This may sound ideal but how can one know what normal means when it comes to our appearance? Everyone is different and unique so why are so many of us obsessed with others and how they look and live. Well, for many this obsession can be a way of life and lead them to seek the perfection they see in someone else's appearance. If we follow this approach to life are we not living our lives for the approval of others, fearful of not being accepted by society?

I am one of the many people who always sought the approval

of others and lived most of my life striving for this and not being true to myself. I believed that I was not 'normal' and that by gaining this recognition from others I would gain 'normal' status and be content.

I am one of the many people who have lived a life of fear and unhappiness. This is not due to anyone else but me and how I viewed myself. I was the one who decided earlier in my life to do whatever it took to be thin. Most people enjoy their lives and have some regrets but they have not wasted half their living years trying to achieve the perfect body. I have always believed that you should control things as much as possible but some things seem to spiral out of our control and into an unknown area. I am one of the many people who have developed anorexia nervosa and bulimia nervosa and will have to try to deal with it and its complications for the rest of my life. So here is my story with all of its ups and downs, from how I developed this disorder to gradually coming to deal with my condition.

WHERE IT ALL BEGAN

I am twenty-four years of age. I am from County Waterford and have lived on a farm in the countryside, which I love, for most of my life. I am from a large family of eight children. I have five brothers and two sisters, who have always been loving and supportive. I was given a great start in life and received a good education. I have great parents who would support my siblings and me in anything we wanted to do. We value life greatly and appreciate the importance of making the most of it. I have a large group of family and friends who have always been there for me. I believe that I am a good listener, outgoing, caring, adventurous and a fairly well-grounded person overall. So where did it all go wrong? When did I begin to hate myself?

I believe that my eating disorder began when I was twelve and in sixth class, in a small rural primary school. I was one of six in my class and was friends with everyone. I loved school and meeting my friends and getting up to all sorts of things as kids do. But I always liked to be in control of things and in many ways was a perfectionist. Everything was normal until I reached puberty and things began to take a turn for the worst. I was always a curious person so I had a fair idea of what was happening to my body and all the changes that I was to experience. In theory it sounded acceptable but in actuality I did not understand the emotional changes that accompanied these physical changes.

As I began to develop so did my figure and my appearance. As I began to put on weight and have more curves, I was called names such as 'baby bulk tank' and 'roly poly'. I had always wanted to be liked by everyone so it was difficult to understand why they would pick on me and call me these names. Now I know they were only being kids and they probably believed that it was their duty to call names and be the tough guys. I found it hard to deal with and did not tell anyone about this and as it slowly became more frequent, I gradually became less accepting of my appearance. I began to feel less happy and more angry about how I looked and also that I could not stand up for myself. I began to question myself, 'Am I too fat? Maybe I should lose weight?'.

I was growing up but I wished that I wasn't because it meant that I would have to deal with big changes, one of which would be leaving primary school and heading to secondary school. This terrified me and probably everyone else in my class but that didn't help me. Even though I had four older brothers who had already crossed this hurdle successfully I was not consoled. I was always a worrier; I worried about everything. Looking back, I think that I did not want to grow up and leave the safe haven that I had been in for eight years but I had no choice, I could not control this and had to just get on with things. I was going to an all-girls' school in the town all on my own as my friends were all heading in different directions, so I would be alone. The notion of being alone was something that always scared me – it still does. I like my independence but being alone is something much more daunting. I would have to take control of myself and just get on with life and not care about others and their views of me. This, however, was easier said than done and so a new stage in my life began: one of confusion, hate, anger, deceit, fear, unhappiness and finally despair. I began to let remarks by others about my body affect my thoughts and the image I had of myself. I started to doubt myself and the changes occurring. I began to hate the weight that I put on, even though it was normal. But I believed that I was getting too big too fast.

That summer was the beginning of something that took control of my life and began to alter the person I was to become. I began to think that I was too fat and that all I had to do was lose a few pounds here and there so that my body did not look so much out of proportion. As a child, I had always liked order. I would have a place for all my toys and many times I would not play with them because it would create a mess, but this was unrealistic in a house of seven other children because they didn't care about my obsessions and played with whatever toys they liked, including mine. So when I wanted to take control of how I looked I knew I could do this on my own without others ruining it for me. I could eat what I wanted and be my own person.

These things gradually began to conflict with one another. As I lost weight people began to question what I was eating and how much I was eating. By the time I began secondary school

I was literally half the person I had been. I felt good about how I looked while always seeking to be thinner. But inside I had many negative emotions that began to eat away at me. I was very confused by these emotions and found it hard to understand why the initial delight I got from losing weight was not always present. It was replaced by feelings of hatred, fear, anger and guilt. I believed that the only way of dealing with how I felt was by not eating. Soon this was how I began to deal with all negative feelings. I would have days of not eating anything at all, living on nothing but fresh air. My life began to revolve around food: how I could avoid it and how I could live without eating anything. I began to want nothing else but to be thin, and was willing to reach my goal at whatever cost, as I felt that this would lead to my ultimate happiness.

Eventually this caught up with me and my parents began to query my eating habits and argue about me and with others at home because I was not eating. The changes in my mentality were also clearly evident to others. My moods and emotions changed drastically as I became preoccupied with my body image. There were major changes in my physical appearance: by now I weighed no more than a young child. My development was stunted. The person my family had known was gone and in her place was a pale, thin, fragile emotional wreck, who was slowly disintegrating in front of their eyes.

Everyone pleaded with me to at but no one had the ability to get through to me as I was convinced that I needed to lose ever more weight in order to like myself. My family feared for my life as I deteriorated but this was something I never worried about because many times I felt that I would be better off dead. When my family's efforts were unsuccessful I was brought to a GP where my mother was given the advice that maybe I should be put on anti-depressants or placed in a psychiatric hospital because I was so irrational and capable of anything, even harming myself and others. This, thank God was not what my mother had in mind as help. Within a few weeks she found a psychologist who dealt with people with eating disorders and so I went. I visited the psychologist every week and began to uncover my feelings but it would take a lot more work than that. This was only the beginning of a very long road that would take years.

In secondary school I made friends slowly and was happy with school but it was too late – I now thought of nothing else but food. Food was the first and last thought I had every day. I hated myself and hated even more the relationship I had with food. Each day seemed like hell: constant fights with my family because I wouldn't eat and then the fights they had with each other about me. My mother was very close to me and we always seemed to have a good relationship. I always wanted to be with her. Slowly this changed and I began to hate everyone. I believed that they only wanted me to get fat and make me unhappy. I believed that happiness could only be achieved through losing weight and being thin. But all that I achieved through my weight loss was unhappiness and misery.

FUN AND GAMES IN MY SCHOOLDAYS

Throughout all my years in secondary school, I had an eating disorder and it was in those years that I realised that weight was a big issue for me but not so much the root of my unhappiness. I tried to live like everyone else my age but this was hard as I had many other issues to overcome. During school, things were mostly normal and my weight issue was not the centre of people's lives, nor was it ever mentioned by anyone. This was something that I was grateful for but I believed that my problem went unnoticed by others. However, looking back, I know that this was totally unrealistic, as everyone had to know that something was wrong just by looking at me.

My teachers treated me like everyone else and I could become involved in all of the activities that I wished. I loved singing and used this as a way to express myself. My friends were great, even though it must have been hard sometimes to be in my company because I was often very withdrawn. They never made an issue of this but they must have had their suspicions. We did our best to enjoy ourselves. In the early years of secondary school my group of friends rarely talked about food but as we got older, it came to be of more interest. I was always good to give my opinion on this topic and expressed the view that diets were never a healthy means of losing weight. I loved school and was determined to do well. My siblings and I used to have to walk half a mile to and from the bus to home. I would use this as a competition: I had to get home first even though all the lads were much taller and faster then me so it was a real struggle to achieve, especially as I was so weak physically. Still, more often than not I achieved my goal.

There were many days I used to go to school crying and in bad form and extremely weak but I never missed a day because it was where I could be free from anyone trying to force me to eat against my will. I did find some things difficult, like lunch break and having to eat in the company of others. Some days I would sit in the bathroom until lunch was over so I wouldn't have to deal with this problem and could avoid food altogether. There were school outings I did not want to go on as I did not know what I would do about eating when everyone else went for chips and fast food One of my biggest fears was having to eat this kind of food, especially in the company of others. I saw what others ate and thought how good they had it: how they could eat what they wanted and still be thin?

AS TIME PASSED

I continued to visit my psychologist and was asked to do various things such as relaxation exercises to try to relax my body. This was so hard as I was always so tense and uptight. I was so bad that I found it so hard to sleep and often woke up early in the mornings, as I believed that sitting or lying down would only make me fat. I would not want to sit in the car and would use my hands to lift me from the seat and prevent me from relaxing. When I was working at weekends and over the summers, I often worked very long days and did double shifts because I could not say 'No'. This also gave me something to be doing and I could stay busy and be paid for it and not have to eat. I could avoid the issue of food and feel somewhat normal in these surroundings.

I also had to record all the food that I ate and how I felt before and after eating it. This seemed pointless as I always seemed to feel the same, I felt sick and bloated after eating and never wanted to eat in the first place. I would have so many emotions going through my mind: guilt, anger, anxiety, fear and of course sadness and disgust. At the earlier stages all that I would eat for dinner were fun-size boxes of cereal, which I felt to be loads – and that was only on good days. I would try where possible to avoid eating anything else. Gradually I began to eat more foods and not be so restricted in my diet. As I began to recover and eat more my moods changed. I began to feel better in myself and believed that things were improving. But it was not so simple.

UPS AND DOWNS

I began to try harder to recover so I began to put on weight because I was eating more. Slowly I began to be happier in school and home. I was allowed to visit the psychologist only every few weeks which gave me some freedom to do what I wanted. But I would return to my old ways of refusing to eat or eating and then getting sick – which was not known by others at this point.

When I was told during one visit to the psychologist that I was not allowed to do PE in school until I put up some weight and kept it at a healthy level for my body type, I was so angry. I felt that I was being deprived of my means of preventing weight gain. I had always loved sport and exercise but as time passed and my anorexia developed, I began to become obsessed with it. I believed that everyone was trying to make me fat. I decided that I had to do something so instead I began to exercise at home. I would often, after eating a meal, go to the bathroom or my room and run on the spot for as long as I could without arousing suspicion, to try to counteract what I had eaten. I also remember times that I would wake at night just so that I could complete some exercise routines lasting thirty to sixty minutes.

RECOVERY: A SLOW PROCESS

As time went on and I began to eat a little more and put on some weight, I was happy for a while but then would think that I was getting too fat as my clothes were getting too tight and I did not know what to do. I had to eat to stay alive but I never wished to get heavy. This was when I began to think of other avenues to stop me getting fat so I tried to hide food in tissues and then find ways of discarding them without others noticing, I gradually started to make myself sick to stop weight gain, and would vomit up what food I could, so I developed bulimia as well as anorexia. I had tried everything to avoid food and as I began to eat, I slowly put on weight. This resulted in me feeling angry with myself for being mentally weak by letting others force me to do something that I was so against. I began to get sick after meals to prevent me getting any fatter and also in a weird way it gave me control of the situation so I was much happier. This, I think, was much worse than not eating as it became a habit and would be much harder to overcome. I would eat what I was given or less and then vomit it up as soon as possible. I used to go to the bathroom as soon as I had finished my meals.

At the beginning I felt great. But as time went on my emotions were mixed. I was happy as I had got rid of the food that everyone believed I had eaten but then I would feel guilty for deceiving my parents while they were spending so much money on my visits to the doctor But I couldn't stop. I had found it to be the only way to deal with how I felt. I was afraid to tell anyone. I felt that they would be really disappointed and that I would have let them down. So I kept my secret to myself. From time to time I got caught out but I denied it completely. I remember the first time that I was asked if I had vomited my meal up. It was as if someone had accused me of murder. I was shocked that my mother had figured out my trick and that others now knew my secret.

EFFECTS THIS DISEASE HAD ON MY LIFE
One day when I was combing my hair (which would have been thick and healthy) as normal, I noticed that there were clumps of hair on my brush. I was stunned that my hair was falling out. This was one of the many side-effects I would have to face because of my eating disorder. On days when I was in extremely bad

form, feeling extremely upset and angry, I would try to pull out my hair, scratch my face and body with my nails, in frustration with others and myself for giving in to them and eating. My nails became brittle and were always breaking with the slightest touch. Another big thing was that my skin was dry and my eyes seemed to be blurry all the time. I was always cold and often would lose feeling in my fingers and toes. My body was weak and I even broke my hand because my bones were so brittle. I constantly had a headache and a pain in my stomach and even when I ate I would feel sick. Another major effect was that my periods stopped for months on end and were never regular. Yet another major effect was that my teeth began to turn off-colour and decay, which I ignored for years. I never believed that this disease would have so many implications.

I tried to help things by eating more and doing what I was advised by my psychologist: to relax and think of other things rather than food and to divert my energy to expressing myself and my emotions in my food diary. It was such a struggle all the time, as it was not something I could just switch off in my mind. Thinking about food was always present and it was as strong as any phobia that people might have, I cried all the time and worried about what eating food would do to me. I worried about its effects on my body. On bad days I would even become aggressive because I was not getting what I wanted and often hit my brothers if they tried to get me to eat.

My fear of food was ever-present. If you could imagine someone having a fear or extreme phobia of things such as spiders or rats, it was like putting me in a room surrounded by food. I would have dreams in which some foods would take the form of a monster which would gradually eat away at my body. I had no means of escaping this nightmare: it was taking over my life both in my sleeping hours and more actively in my daily life. I would often have days when I was so weak that my heart would race. Things seemed to be always getting worse. I had to decide that I needed to try and change them and try to help myself – if not for me then for my family. They did not deserve this.

I often wished that I was dead or that I would just be allowed to die. Some days I even thought of how I could make this happen even though, unknown to myself, I was gradually losing myself to my illness and slowly dying. My days were full of anguish and despair I believed that my life was not worth living and that everything that I did was pointless. I was always a self-conscious person and as things worse I had very low self-esteem and a bad self-image. I was always worried about how others perceived me and would look at people and wish that I had their lives. I had to try to overcome this otherwise I would never be able to reach the goals that I had for my life. I wanted to become a teacher or something in that line and to have a family of my own and be successful.

One of the things that made me begin to question what I was doing to my body occurred when I was about sixteen. I had not had a period in a few years and my younger sister, who was eleven, had got hers. I was so angry with her and I would not talk to her as I was jealous of how she was growing up. Even though I was always a mature person, my physical development was stunted. Thinking back I feel guilty for being unsupportive and completely self-absorbed. This incident got me thinking about myself and I remember the doctor telling me that I had already reduced my chances greatly and that every day I lived like this I lessened my chances of ever having a family of my own. When I was very young I loved playing with dolls and always had to play the mammy and now this disease could prevent me ever making it a reality. I think that this glimpse of the future got me thinking and I had to try to be honest with myself about the damage that I was doing to my body.

FAMILY LIFE

My anorexia and bulimia had a major effect on my family and my relationship with them. For most of my teenage years I would not talk to them because I hated everyone else as well as myself. I only remember arguing with them and I believe that I missed all the normal everyday things that most families enjoy. I would not allow myself to speak to them about anything and withdrew myself from their lives, which led me to become wrapped up in my own life. I never wanted to join in at different events. I could not think about anything other than food and how I looked. As I mentioned previously, I am from a big family so prior to my developing an eating disorder we would always have done things together and enjoyed one another's company. Even when we fought the anger would never last too long. This, however, changed with the development of my eating disorder and I began to believe that no one wanted to talk to me. I lost the closeness I once had with my siblings.

I was the fifth youngest and the eldest girl in the family so I often took on the role of mammy. I loved to feel as if I was helping, as I admired my mother greatly and I used her in many ways as a role model. I would do the same work that she did and liked to have responsibility. I would cook the meals and do what I could to help around the house but as I got sick things began to change. I tried to do everything for my brothers and sisters. I tried to take on all the responsibilities of a mother. My mother was a great woman and had so much to do that I felt that I should help out in any way I could. I felt I had to be responsible for everything and everyone in the world.

My brother, who was a year older than me, also began to show signs of an eating disorder. He became picky about his food, so I would make things for him that I knew he would eat. Thinking back I was probably afraid of what could happen to him and this was his reaction to my sickness. I remember my parents giving out and shouting at him for behaving like this, asking, 'Do you want to be sick too and turn out like Bríd?' This was not to make me feel bad but to make him see sense and to see the damage he would cause himself if he continued in this way.

My parents always tried their best to give us a good upbringing, to help us appreciate what we had and to respect others and ourselves. My illness, however, took its toll on everyone. My father was traditional in his ideas and often found it hard to understand what was happening to his once bubbly daughter. He was sometimes driven to shout at me and even tried to force me to eat, in the hope that I would realise the damage I was doing to myself. He did not understand my illness but did his best to deal with it and sort it out...

My mother was different. She knew what I was like, that I was a very determined person, and that anything I set my mind to do I could achieve. She tried a different approach and would ask me to tell her what I would like to eat and get it for me. But this had no effect either.

Very quickly I got sick and seemed to deteriorate fast. The mood in the home seemed to decline with me and there were lots of arguments that were all rooted in my illness. I withdrew from my siblings and began to think that they hated me, just like everyone else. My parents argued about me all the time because they could not get through to me. They were at their wit's end. Even as I began to get help and we all began to acknowledge that

I had a problem, the house still seemed to be full of tension.

When I was writing this story I asked my family how my illness had affected them. One of my sisters told me that it was really hard for her as she had always looked up to me and now I was not there for her or anyone. They all felt helpless and often this affected decisions they made such as having friends over or going away with friends. They felt as if they had lost the sister they once knew and she had become possessed by some evil but dominant power. My sister also told me that one day my brother and she were driven to such worry they asked our mother, with uncontrollable tears, if I was going to die and what could they do. My mother could not give a consoling answer as she lived every day in the fear that I might possibly die. For an eight-year-old child the worry of watching someone slowly kill herself is unimaginable.

RECOVERY

I seemed to take a toll on everyone's lives and felt responsible for things going wrong. This was something that always affected me and now I knew that I was really causing trouble for others. I felt as if my life was a burden to others and that I had to try and do something about it. I was losing myself to my eating disorder and I needed to try to overcome how I felt.

I now had to be honest with myself and also with those who were trying to help me get over this disease. Being honest was probably one of the hardest things for me to do. Even though I knew that my life was not normal and that I was not like everyone else my age, I did not really ever admit aloud that I had something wrong with me.

My recovery was long as I had many obstacles to overcome. There were many times when I seemed to be recovering but something would trigger something in my brain and I would be back in the darkness of the disease. But it seemed to me to gradually become easier. I could get a glimpse of normality the many times I was doing well and I could sense that there was a better way of life for me beyond my bulimia. I think that my bulimia had become like a safe place that I could go to when things got difficult. I would describe it as a habit that is very easy to get into but much harder to get out of. I began to be happier with my life and little by little overcame my disorder. My eating became more regular and vomiting less frequent but it never stopped for long periods, which was still a secret to others.

In my Leaving Cert year things were going well and I was steadily recovering but after the exams I went away to work for the summer and I stayed away from home. This was the first time that I had such freedom and could live independently. I believed that I could get by without help from others and do all the things that I wanted to do. I enjoyed the experience of being away from home but the worry of exams and of the debs quickly began to take control. I began to let my worries take over and I began to feel less confident about myself. During this period I slowly retreated back into my old ways and with no one to watch over me I lost weight and began to vomit again.

While I was home for a few days my mother became anxious about me and decided that I needed to get some help again. So I had to surrender my freedom and accept that I might not be able to get over this so fast. It had taken me seven years and I was still controlled by my bulimia. I wanted to get over it so badly and to be like others my age and go out socialising. I had to be able to deal with college life and not let my bulimia take away my hopes of a career.

Many times things began to improve but after a while the old me would reappear. I was never sure if I was rid of the disease. I was still worried about my weight but I really needed to block it out of my mind as much as possible and to get on with things.

I received my results and got the course that I wanted, I got over the debs and things were getting brighter. I was beginning to become much more confident and could now see that I was capable of doing things on my own and achieving my goals. For the first time in years, I could see light at the end of the tunnel.

I went to college in Dublin in September 2001, which of course worried my family but they had to allow me to grow up and face reality. Many of my relatives had little faith in my being able to cope but my parents were adamant that I had to get on with things and go to Dublin or anywhere else I thought I should go. They knew that I was responsible and able to look after myself and I could not allow food to control my life forever. I made friends in college and I experienced the joys of student life. I was slowly beginning to socialise and get more involved in different college events. I had to begin to take responsibility for myself and be independent. I loved my course and my college was small and therefore not daunting. I was enjoying my life and appreciating it. I was able to see outside the box and look towards the future.

It took more than a few days or weeks for things get better. Even though I relapsed many times these relapses were still part of me getting over my disease. Each time I relapsed I had to deal with another underlying issue within myself that I had believed insignificant. I could only take each day as it came and could never be sure of what might be ahead of me but I began to see that it was no good worrying and trying to control everything.

Throughout the four years of college I enjoyed a fairly good life. Things were normal and I slowly began to control my life and my eating disorder. I began to believe that I had no other choice if I wanted the chance of a prosperous life controlled by my achievements and not by how I looked. I had to be strong and accept the life I was given and not be ungrateful or feel unworthy of it. I could see that I had as much potential as everyone else and that I was no less worthy of happiness or love.

I had bad days and weeks but I learned to control them to the extent that I could get on with things. During these times I returned for counselling to get a perspective on things and also to not let things go back to the way they were.

The relationship that I had with my family slowly improved and when I would come home at weekends I would be able to chat and talk about everyday things that did not include food. I could see that I was improving and so could they but it had taken the best part of twelve years of my life and also of theirs. I still found it hard to even talk about my disease and how it had affected them but things were beginning to progress.

THINGS CAN ONLY GET BETTER

It was never easy to overcome my eating disorders but I had to learn to deal with things on my own and not to relate problems or worries to food. This problem is ever-present in me and will be until I die but I have learned to deal with it. I have to try every day not to let myself return to that vicious circle of negative images and attitudes about myself. As I recover I feel more confident being myself in society for and confident that I can be happy, and thankful for all I have. I have to find new avenues other than food to vent my frustration and anger, such as walking, running, music.

I can now see that I cannot bear the worries of the world on my shoulders as I had done for years. I must see that I am not responsible for everything and even in my own family I cannot solve all problems. Everyone needs to take responsibility for themselves, me included. I do not blame anyone for what has happened but feel that it is only an outward expression of how you feel within.

It is also only in the last year that I have begun to talk about my eating disorder and have begun to ask about what I was like to live with because I have very little memory of my life for most of my teenage years. I have let myself block it from my mind. In many ways, I wish that I could recall some of the incidents that showed my unstable mind. The effects that an eating disorder can have on one's life are frightening. I was startled to hear what I was like and told my mother that I would have hated to live with me. I seem to have blocked from my mind any major incident during the years I was unwell.

It is also only in the last year that my relationship with most of my family has really improved and we talk, argue, and socialise like any normal family. I missed out on a lot of experiences throughout my childhood by giving over twelve years of my life to feelings of depression and unhappiness. I have had to make a choice, just as I did earlier in my life. Even though life is full of obstacles, I can get over them by availing of the support and help that surrounds me, and not by returning to food as a means of channelling my anxieties.

I am now much more open to talking about how I feel and can admit to having both anorexia and bulimia, which was very difficult, but has helped me learn a lot about myself. I have begun to deal with the issues that arose due to my eating disorder. One major obstacle was visiting the dentist, I spent years avoiding dentists in order not to admit to my problem, which was something that I did not want others to know. But

I have taken the plunge by making the visit and feel extremely proud of myself because I faced one of my fears on my own. It is possible to get over an eating disorder and live an enjoyable and fulfilling life. I am glad that I have taken control of my life and can now have the chance to become someone I can be proud of.

I still have days that I feel crap and anxious. I find it hard to motivate myself. I still worry about how I look and what others think but try not to allow it to rule me as I am becoming more confident in myself. I do believe that I can achieve complete recovery, which I have not yet done. Even though I have dealt with and have overcome both anorexia and bulimia, I still have steps to take. I can see the effects that the disorder has had on my body and my life and do not want to surrender anymore to it. I find that bulimia is more difficult to overcome as it is like a habit that I have formed and is difficult to break, as it seems to have the ability to re-emerge when things get me down.

My body has had a lot to deal with over the past thirteen years and I cannot know the extent of the damage until it surfaces. All I can do, however, is take each day at a time and take care of myself from now on.

I hope to one day have a family of my own and will do my best to be a success in all aspects of life but only time will tell. All you can do is live each day as it comes, deal with each difficult day and hope to come out smiling.

It is only in the last year that I am beginning to live my life the way I want to. I can now see all that I have missed out on from having an eating disorder. I also feel that I have learned to be much more open-minded and see life in a positive light. I feel that this quotation from Katherine Mansfield sums up this part of my life: 'I have made it a rule of my life never to regret and never to look back. Regret is an appalling waste of energy…you can't build on it; it's only good for wallowing in.'

I have been given a second chance to make the most of life. I have learned so much about myself over my years of recovery and hope that I can continue to enjoy life without too many regrets and appreciate how precious it is.

Goethe wrote: 'The soul must see through these eyes alone, and if they are dim, the whole world is clouded.' I now try to have a positive outlook on life and don't take my health for granted. I feel that I have wasted too much of my life already to worry and misery. It is only now I am seeing the world in a new light, one of hope. I now try each day to have a positive outlook on things. We are all responsible for our own destiny and we must enjoy life while we can. Life is what you make it. Therefore, it is only I who can determine how happy and successful I am. One of my inspirations is the quotation from the American philosopher Thoreau: 'Go confidently in the direction of your dreams! Live the life you've imagined.'

I am very grateful to my family for believing in me and putting so much time and energy into getting me back. I know that if it had not been for their love and support I would not be as well as I am now: I would have let my illness rule my life.

Resources

Dr Gillian Moore-Groarke, 5A, Block B, Harley Court, Sarsfield Road, Wilton, Cork. Registered consultant psychologist with a special interest in the area of eating disorders, health psychology, pain management and stress management. Tel/fax: 021-4343073. www.irishpsychology.com

Eating Disorder Unit, St Patrick's Hospital, James's Street, Dublin 8. Large in-patient unit in Ireland for the treatment of anorexia nervosa and bulimia. Tel: 01-2493200. www.stpatrickshosp.com

Overeaters Anonymous, PO Box 2529, Dublin 5. Offers a programme of recovery from compulsive overeating using Twelve Steps and Twelve Traditions of Overeaters Anonymous. Tel: 01-2788106.

Body Whys, Central Office, PO Box 105, Blackrock, County Dublin. National charity which offers help, support and understanding for people with eating disorders, their families and friends. Tel: (LoCall) 1890-200444. www.bodywhys.ie

Irish Medical Directory, PO Box 5049, Dublin 6. Comprehensive and widely-used guide to health care and the medical profession in Ireland. Telephone: 01-4926040. www.imd.ie

Irish Society of Homeopaths, 25-27 Dominick Street, Galway. Representative body for professional homeopaths in Ireland. Tel/Fax: 091-565040. www.irishsocietyofhomeopaths.com

Irish Association for Counselling and Therapy, 8 Cumberland Street, Dun Laoghaire, County Dublin. Establishes, maintains and regulates standards for the profession of counselling and therapy in Ireland. Tel: 01-2300061. www.irish-counselling.ie

Psychological Society of Ireland, CX House, 2A Corn Exchange Place, Dublin 2. Professional body for psychologists in Ireland which aims to advance psychology as a pure and applied science in Ireland and elsewhere. Tel: 01-6717122. www.psihq.ie

The British Psychological Society, St Andrew's House, 48 Princess Road East, Leicester LE1 7DR. Representative body for psychologists and psychology in the UK. Tel: 0044-116-2549568/ fax 0044-116-2470787. www.bps.org.uk

Irish Patients Association Ltd., Unit 1, First Floor, 24 Church Road, Ballybrack, County Dublin. Aims to place patients at the centre of healthcare, improve the quality and service they receive, improve cost effectiveness, improve the availability of service and protect present and future patients' rights. Tel: 01-2722555

SUGGESTED READING

Anderson A., L. Cohn and T. Holbrook (2000) *Making Weight: Men's Conflicts with Food, Weight, Shape and Appearance.* Gurze.

Bodywhys. (2006) *Binge Eating – Breaking the Cycle: a Self-Help Guide towards Recovery.*

Bovey, S. (1994) *The Forbidden Body.* Pandora.

Buckroyd J. (1994) *Eating Your Heart Out.* Optima.

Curwen B., S. Palmer and P. Ruddel. (2000) *Brief Cognitive Behaviour Therapy.* Safe Publications.

Fairburn C.G. (1995) *Overcoming Binge Eating.* The Guildford Press.

Greenberger D. and C. Padesky. (1995) *Mind Over Mood.* The Guildford Press.

Hamachek, D.E. (1978) 'Psychodynamics of Normal and Neurotic Perfectionism'. *Psychology* 15 27-33.

Hirschman J. R. and C. Munter. (1996) *Overcoming Overeating.* Cedar.

Moore-Groarke G. and T. Nerney. (2004) *Watch your Weight – a Quality of Life Approach.* Mercier Press

Madders, J. (1993) *Stress and Relaxation, Self-Help Techniques for Everyone.* Optima.

Moore-Groarke, G. and S. Thompson. (1995) *When Food Becomes Your Enemy.* Mercier Press

Roth G. (1986) *Breaking Free from Compulsive Eating.* Signet.

Rowe, D. (1986) *Depression and the Way out of Your Prison.* Routledge.

Rowe, D. (1996) *The Successful Self.* Harper Collins.

Treasure J. and U. Schmidt. (1996) *Getting Better Bite by Bite.* Psychology Press.

Binge/Compulsive eating workbook for Kids and Teens, downloadable from www.growthcentral.com

Useful Websites

www.aso.org.uk
www.aweightout.com
www.bchealthguide.org
www.bodywhys.ie
www.clinicalevidence.com
www.counselling-directory.org.uk
www.epigee.org/mental_health/anorexia.html
www.ezinearticles.com www.healthyplace.com
www.growthcentral.com
www.healthpromotion.ie
www.irish-counselling.ie
www.irishhealth.com
www.irishpsychology.com
www.malehealth.co.uk
www.myselfhelp.com
www.ontario.cmha.ca
www.rcpsych.ac.uk/mentalhealthinformation/therapies/
cognitivebehaviouraltherapy
www.vhi.ie
www.webmd.com